PRA

RAISING BOYS WHO RESPECT GIRLS

"I am thrilled for Dave's newest book. This will help us guide our sons into healthy relationships with girls. That's what we all want but may not have known how. In this #MeToo era, this book, from a respected thought-leader, pastor, and father of four sons, is exactly what we need to teach our sons to honor and defend women, without diminishing healthy masculinity. Let's all raise a generation of men who respect women."

—SHAUNTI FELDHAHN, SOCIAL RESEARCHER AND BESTSELLING AUTHOR OF *FOR WOMEN ONLY* AND *FOR PARENTS ONLY*

"As a father of two boys I want to instill in them the exact lesson learned from this book. The challenge for all of us is that raising boys into men who treat women with respect is not something that automatically happens. In this book you'll discover not just the 'how' but also the ability to teach your children the 'why.' As a bonus, Dave's writing is infectious and his instruction is courageous. He is absolutely the right author to deliver this message. If you are a father of boys (or girls) you will not regret reading this book!"

—BRENT EVANS, PRESIDENT, MARRIAGETODAY AND FOUNDER, XOMARRIAGE.COM

"Our culture sends mixed and harmful messages about what it means to be a man. As a father of two sons, it has been a constant battle to help them avoid internalizing these destructive ideas. That's why I'm thankful for Dave Willis's book. It will help parents equip their sons to have a biblical, redemptive vision of manhood."

—JIM DALY, PRESIDENT, FOCUS ON THE FAMILY

"As a survivor of child abuse and domestic violence, one of my greatest dreams for my daughters is that God blesses them with loving, gentle, and honorable husbands. Reading *Raising Boys Who Respect Girls* has given me profound hope for our children's generation. The humble, compassionate, and poignant words of Dave Willis provide a beautiful window into the heart of a father who desires—not only to raise his own sons to model Jesus—but to inspire other parents to do the same. Rather than shame masculinity, Dave elevates it as a blessing from God to be celebrated and used to model Jesus Christ. I am grateful for this book."

—JENNIFER GREENBERG, AUTHOR OF *NOT FORSAKEN: A STORY OF LIFE AFTER ABUSE*

"Many modern-day cultural critics both inside and outside the church are standing on the banks of a river complaining about all the trash flowing downstream. Much of the critique is around the state of masculinity. One of the greatest needs of the day is for men and women to move upstream and stop the trash from being thrown in the river to begin with. My firm belief is that the upstream issue of our day is the hearts of men. Dave Willis has journeyed upstream not only to identify the problem but to give us practical solutions. The health of a church, a community, and a culture can never exceed the health of the hearts of its men."

—SCOTT NICKELL, TEACHING PASTOR, SOUTHLAND CHRISTIAN CHURCH; COHOST, THE *LOCKER ROOM PODCAST*

"This isn't about toxic masculinity or the gender wars. *Raising Boys Who Respect Girls* is about the quiet, seemingly unnoticeable things that happen every day that perpetuate the mind-set that women are not worthy of love and respect. With bold honesty and conviction, Willis shares his own past mistakes, his current fight to end the cycle with his four boys, and practical advice we can all implement as we work toward a changed future."

—AMANDA LUEDEKE, VICE PRESIDENT AND AGENT AT MACGREGOR & LUEDEKE

"Dave Willis is an anointed speaker and writer. No matter where you are in your parenting walk, you need to read this book."

—DR. SCOTT AND LEAH SILVERII, AUTHORS OF *LIFE AFTER DIVORCE* AND *UNCUFFED: BULLET PROOFING LAW ENFORCEMENT MARRIAGES*

"Dave Willis boldly tackles topics that are imperative to address with all men, young and old alike. His direct and courageous transparency, both through personal experience and candid interviews, unveils and illuminates root patterns continuing to keep women in bondage. Dave powerfully reveals the hidden struggles and calls the next generation of men to more. *Raising Boys Who Respect Girls* is a must-have resource for anyone parenting boys."

—LAUREN REITSEMA, AUTHOR; VICE PRESIDENT OF STRATEGY AND COMMUNICATIONS, THE CENTER FOR RELATIONSHIP EDUCATION

"This book is for every parent who cares about raising boys in our day. Dave helps us understand the challenges of raising 'men of honor' in a complicated and confusing culture. He shares his own struggles with his signature humor and practical style that gives do-able answers that every mom and dad need. Do yourself and your boys a favor and read this book today!"

—GARRETT BOOTH, PASTOR, GRACE HOUSTON

"Those who mistakenly believe it is impossible to be effective as a parent or guardian know nothing about *Raising Boys Who Respect Girls*! Anyone who has concerns about raising children needs this book in their personal library. Dave's keen dedication for his family leaves an everlasting impression about the delightful measures of raising respectable boys. Dynamic! Pulsating with spiritual energy . . . waiting to be read!"

—KIMBERLY BAXTER-LEE, M.ED, ADMINISTRATOR, CHARLES HENRY TERRELL ACADEMY; PROFESSOR OF HISTORY, PAINE COLLEGE

"More than ever before, our sons need to know what a real man is . . . and what he isn't. As a mom of four sons I am passionate about raising my boys to become good and godly men, yet the culture we are raising them in can make that really hard. Oh, how desperately we need a voice of reason to help families catch a vision for raising boys to be true men—men of character and integrity. Men who respect women. In the pages of this book, Dave Willis offers that voice of reason—and what a better world this would be if all parents raising boys could read it."

—MONICA SWANSON, AUTHOR, *BOY MOM*; HOST, *THE BOY MOM PODCAST*; BLOGGER AT MONICASWANSON.COM

"The tone Dave sets in this book is one of truth and grace. It doesn't bash men or parents, it brings realization to why things are the way they are. I truly believe that anyone who reads this book will have the power to help change the direction of our culture. It's a book I had no idea I had been waiting for, until I read it."

—Barclay Bishop, journalist and network TV news anchor

"Boys need role models to show them what real manhood looks like, which includes relating to girls in an honorable way—not objectifying or discounting them. Willis compels parents to bring an end to the disrespect of females and the belittling of males, through poignant illustrations, sobering statistics, and a hopeful way forward. As parents of three boys and two girls, we are deeply grateful for this timely, transparent resource. We highly recommend this right-now message to anyone who is raising or impacting the next generation."

—Adam Reid, lead pastor, Central Michigan Christian Church; and Katie M. Reid, author, *Made Like Martha*; parents to five great kids (ages 3 to 15)

"This is the most important book I have read in quite some time. Dave Willis speaks biblically, yet frankly, about the global problem of raising boys who respect girls. This boy mom couldn't put it down. It's a must-read!"

—Amber Lia, bestselling coauthor, *Triggers* and *Parenting Scripts*

"*Raising Boys Who Respect Girls* is a much-needed reality check, reminding us that it takes the utmost courage, perseverance, and intention to raise children who are willing to go against the loud voice of culture. But the most important reminder is that a life of respect has to begin with each and every one of us, as we lead our children by example. I'm grateful for the bold truth in this hopeful book!"

—Debra Fileta, MA, LPC, author, *Choosing Marriage*; creator, TrueLoveDates.com

"*Raising Boys Who Respect Girls* might be one of the most important books I've ever read. As a dad to four boys, I feel a deep-seated burden to raise young men who will honor and respect women. The crisis is real and the challenges of today make this book so relevant. Willis helps the reader follow the example of Christ in the way He elevated and treated women. I can't wait to go through this book with my sons and with other dads and their sons."

—SCOTT KEDERSHA, DIRECTOR OF MARRIAGE
    MINISTRY, WATERMARK COMMUNITY CHURCH;
    AUTHOR, *READY OR KNOT? 12 CONVERSATIONS EVERY
    COUPLE NEEDS TO HAVE BEFORE MARRIAGE*

"This book is essential to our time. Dave doesn't hold back, bringing honest, researched truth combined with passionate heart. The input from women only makes this resource all the more valuable. The spiritual truth with practical wisdom creates a clinically sound yet such an easy-to-read resource for more than just parents of boys. This book will shift cultural thinking."

—CASSIE REID, PH.D., LPC, SUPERVISOR DIRECTOR OF
    THE MASTER IN MARRIAGE AND FAMILY THERAPY
    PROGRAM, THE KING'S UNIVERSITY AT GATEWAY

RAISING BOYS WHO
RESPECT GIRLS

RAISING BOYS
WHO RESPECT GIRLS

Upending Locker Room Mentality, Blind Spots,
and Unintended Sexism

DAVE WILLIS

NELSON
BOOKS

An Imprint of Thomas Nelson

Published in Nashville, Tennessee, by Nelson Books, an imprint of Thomas Nelson. Nelson Books and Thomas Nelson are registered trademarks of HarperCollins Christian Publishing, Inc.

The author is represented by MacGregor & Luedeke.

Thomas Nelson titles may be purchased in bulk for educational, business, fund-raising, or sales promotional use. For information, please email SpecialMarkets@ThomasNelson.com.

Any Internet addresses, phone numbers, or company or product information printed in this book are offered as a resource and are not intended in any way to be or to imply an endorsement by Thomas Nelson, nor does Thomas Nelson vouch for the existence, content, or services of these sites, phone numbers, companies, or products beyond the life of this book.

Unless otherwise indicated, all Scripture quotations are taken from the Holy Bible, New Living Translation, copyright © 1996, 2004, 2015 by Tyndale House Foundation. Used by permission of Tyndale House Publishers, Inc., Carol Stream, Illinois 60188. All rights reserved.

Scripture quotations marked NIV are taken from the Holy Bible, New International Version®, NIV®. Copyright © 1973, 1978, 1984, 2011 by Biblica, Inc.™ Used by permission of Zondervan. All rights reserved worldwide. www.zondervan.com. The "NIV" and "New International Version" are trademarks registered in the United States Patent and Trademark Office by Biblica, Inc.™

Scripture quotations marked ESV are from the ESV® Bible (The Holy Bible, English Standard Version®), copyright © 2001 by Crossway, a publishing ministry of Good News Publishers. Used by permission. All rights reserved.

ISBN 978-1-4002-1513-3 (eBook)
ISBN 978-1-4002-1509-6 (TP)

Library of Congress Cataloging-in-Publication Data

Names: Willis, Dave, 1978- author.
Title: Raising boys who respect girls : upending locker room mentality,
   blind spots, and unintended sexism / Dave Willis.
Description: Nashville : Thomas Nelson, 2019. | Includes bibliographical
   references.
Identifiers: LCCN 2019008131 (print) | ISBN 9781400215096 (pbk.)
Subjects: LCSH: Child rearing--Religious aspects--Christianity. |
   Parenting--Religious aspects--Christianity. | Men (Christian theology) |
   Sex--Religious aspects--Christianity. | Man-woman
   relationships--Religious aspects--Christianity.
Classification: LCC BV4529 .W576 2019 (print) | LCC BV4529 (ebook) | DDC
   248.8/45--dc23
LC record available at https://lccn.loc.gov/2019008131
LC ebook record available at https://lccn.loc.gov/2019980296

Printed in the United States of America

19 20 21 22 23 LSC 5 4 3 2 1

This book is dedicated to my extraordinary sons:
Cooper, Connor, Chandler, and Chatham.
I love you, and I'm so proud of you.
I know you'll grow to become men worthy of great respect,
and as you grow, may you always be
respecters and protectors of women.

CONTENTS

INTRODUCTION

M y thirteen-year-old son, Cooper, came home from his
first day of eighth grade with a look of bewilderment
on his face. My wife, Ashley, and I immediately started pep-
pering him with questions about his first day, and he mumbled
a few short answers as he checked his phone. Like most adolescent boys, he seemed much more interested in getting to
his video games than he was in carrying on a conversation
about school.

We bribed him with some snacks to keep the conversation going, and before he finished the last bite of pepperoni
Hot Pocket, he asked us one question that nearly left us both
speechless. He cleared his throat and shuffled his feet a bit as
he searched for the words, and then he finally blurted out, "Do
girls like it when boys send them pictures of their penises?"

As you can imagine, this question sparked some immedi-
ate follow-up questions from us. We tried not to act shocked,
because we've found that the calmer we stay the more the boys
will tell us. The moment we freak out, they shut down. We

played it cool and kept asking questions, which finally revealed that some of the boys on his bus had been taking pictures of their genitalia and showing the pictures to the other kids on the bus and also texting those images to other kids.

One boy was flashing a picture and laughing while saying, "Girls love getting these pictures texted to them!"

The boy tried to put his phone right in front of Cooper's face, but Cooper pushed the phone away and made it clear that he had no interest in participating. Our son was shocked by this kind of behavior, but he was also perplexed by that brazen boy's statement. *Do girls really like it when guys do that? Is this actually how relationships are supposed to work?*

We told Cooper that he had done the right thing by standing up to this kind of obscene behavior, and Ashley reassured him that, "No, I can promise you that girls certainly do not like receiving pictures like this. They might giggle out of shock or nervousness, but inside they'll be disgusted, offended, and possibly even terrified. Boys should always treat girls with respect, and what these boys are doing is both disrespectful and illegal."

You might be picturing the boys on this bus as a police lineup of hardened criminals, but these kids come mostly from intact, stable, highly educated, and affluent families. This bus route serviced upper-middle-class neighborhoods and a good number of gated communities. The area has an incredibly low crime rate and is considered one of the best school districts in the state. I realized then that if this kind of behavior was happening in our community, chances are good that it's happening everywhere.

This incident with Cooper is one of the countless incidents that sent me on a quest to find answers and try to become a small part of the solution to the widespread mistreatment, objectification, and disrespect of females. As news stories featuring women being abused started appearing more frequently, they also fueled this journey. Every encounter with injustice kept spurring me onward. The more I researched, the more I became convinced that the problem is even bigger than we've realized, and the solution can be found only in properly equipping the next generation.

As parents and educators of boys, you and I have the influence and the responsibility to teach the next generation of men how to respect themselves and how to respect the next generation of women. I'm not writing this as a guy who has all the answers. I'm inviting you on a journey where we might end up with more questions than answers, but it's a journey that could have profound, positive effects for our children and their children for generations to come. Above all else, I'm just a dad who wants to raise boys who respect girls and who grow up to be men who deeply respect women.

If you're a father of boys, take this journey with me, and together we can have some man-to-man talks about how to raise our sons to be men of integrity and how we can be men of integrity too. This journey can help you and your son(s) grow closer together by sparking some deep and meaningful conversations. I'm hoping the same happens for my sons and me.

If you're a mother of boys, I hope I can peel back the curtain and help you understand the thought process of your son(s). Understanding his masculine mental wiring will be essential in this journey. Raising boys who respect girls doesn't mean we need to demonize or belittle masculinity. On the contrary, we'll be helping our sons reclaim true manhood when we teach them how to respect true womanhood. This journey will help you grow closer to your son(s) by fostering a mutual understanding and opening new lines of communication.

A few quick disclaimers and instructions: First, you need to know that this journey will be full of surprises. The book will most likely not be what you're expecting, and I'm probably not who you'd expect to write a book on this subject. The best journeys in life are usually the unexpected ones.

This book is not a call to progressivism or conservatism. It's not intended to be a political statement, because we put too much stock in politics and politicians to bring real change that only a transformed heart can bring. The ideas and ideals you'll read might sound radical at times, but the teachings and bold, countercultural actions of Jesus seemed radical enough for the establishment of his day to want him executed. As a follower of Christ, if we don't sound a little bit radical at times, we might be missing the point.

This book will not try to shame boys for being males. Boys are awesome! I'm proud to have sons, and I want my sons and yours to attain the highest ideals of authentic manhood. Sadly, many modern boys and men are carrying a broken view of manhood and a broken view of themselves in general. In the well-researched recent book *The Boy Crisis*, the authors point out some staggering trends in modern views of masculinity. They suggest that the recent bombardment of news stories depicting men and boys behaving badly have caused many boys to feel ashamed of their gender and many parents-to-be to disproportionately hope for baby daughters instead of baby sons.[1]

I certainly want to call boys and men to a high standard, but I have no desire to shame boys for being male or to attempt to deconstruct modern manhood and replace it with a more feminized or gender-neutral vision of manhood. On the contrary, I want to recapture the timeless, biblical ideals of manhood. I want to live them out in my own life and teach my sons to do the same. Crimes against women won't stop because men reject the idea of manhood; women will finally be treated with respect when males embrace authentic manhood.

Real men respect women. I know there's a lot of controversy and confusion around what being a "real man" means, and I'll spend a good bit of time unpacking those concepts in later chapters. But, while my message about manhood will come from personal experience and social research, it will also have its foundations in the Bible, which might surprise some readers. The Bible isn't an archaic, rigid manual filled with misogyny, but rather it is the book that holds the solutions we need. I also believe Jesus Christ is the source and embodiment of all truth. I will argue that he did more during his lifetime to advance, recognize, and respect women than anyone else in history.

You don't have to share my faith in Christ to benefit from these principles, but your knowing that I'm writing from a biblical, Christ-centered worldview provides important context.

If you have a mind-set that Christianity and respect for women are somehow incompatible, I hope to completely change your opinion. Whether a Christian or not, please read the chapter entitled "Jesus, Respecter of Women." It might be the most important chapter in this book and might permanently alter some of your paradigms (like Jesus continues to alter my own paradigms).

If you're a fellow Christian reading this, I need to warn you that this book isn't what you'd normally find in the Christian section of the bookstore. I'm going to be blunt at times and use specific words (especially when referring to sex) that might make you turn fifty shades of red. I'm not doing this for shock value, but too many of my fellow Christian writers have whitewashed and watered down these issues out of fear of offending. Sometimes the blunt and specific truth is the only way to adequately communicate.

Let's stop dancing around these issues and have some straight talk. Please stick with me and keep an open mind, even if some of the stories you read make you squirm a bit. I assure you that I'm as uncomfortable as anyone with the levels of bluntness I felt were necessary in certain sections. We'll get through it together and hopefully learn some valuable insights along the way.

The format of this book includes plenty of facts and stats, but it is primarily made up of stories. If you continue reading past the introduction, you'll soon discover that I love telling stories. I believe it's how we learn best. Some of the stories in the coming pages are fictional allegories, but most are true in a factual sense. When appropriate, I've changed the names and other identifying details to protect the anonymity of the people involved.

In my stories you'll probably also see that I have a quirky and sometimes irreverent sense of humor. This is just how I'm wired. I try to never take myself too seriously, but please know I don't take this subject lightly. The humor is intended to keep you engaged and entertained and is never meant to diminish the significance of the subject at hand. I also apologize in advance for any cringe-worthy "dad joke" puns. I'm a dad. I can't help it sometimes.

I should also probably tell you that I'm not a psychologist, a doctorate-degree-wielding expert in this field, or a talking head on cable news. This book will be more unorthodox (and, hopefully, more entertaining) than if one of those guys had written it. I do have a master's degree in a social science field, years of experience in youth and college ministry, and plenty of experience as a dad, but I'm admittedly an outsider when it comes to this subject. Please extend me grace, and remember every great movement has been fueled, at least in part, from unlikely voices and outsiders.

I also need to confess an important fact that I hope doesn't make me lose all credibility with you on this subject. This might shock you, so I'd encourage you to sit down before you learn this shocking revelation . . . I'm a man. That's right, I'm a dude.

Maybe you're offended by the thought of a man writing a book on this subject, because you think it only reaffirms the patriarchal patterns that created these problems in the first place. If you're in that camp, I certainly don't want to patronize you or discredit your convictions. But I'd also encourage you to recognize that men have been a big part of creating this problem, so we need the opportunity to be a part of creating the solutions. That's not chauvinism or feminism; I think that's just common sense.

As a way to give women "the final word" on the topics I'll be addressing, I'm ending each chapter with quotes curated from women and girls of all ages. Most of these quotes were given in response to a request I made on social media. On my public channels, I posted this:

> Ladies, I'm writing a book on how to raise boys who respect girls, and I need your insights. Please share your experiences. What do men and boys do to make you feel respected, and what do men and boys do to make you feel disrespected? Please also share any stories of past abuse or mistreatment that you'd be willing to publicly post, plus any additional perspective you believe might be helpful. I'll share some of these quotes in my book. Thank you!

I'm thankful for the hundreds of ladies who responded. I'm especially inspired by the courageous women who were willing to publicly share their harrowing accounts of past abuse. This book, as well as my own perspective, is much richer because of their courage, wisdom, and insights. I've also included quotes from boys and men of various ages, and their experiences have also greatly enriched my perspective and the message of this book.

In the "In Women's Own Words" sections at the end of each chapter, I've included an age along with a first name and last initial in each quote as a way to give context about each woman's life experience. The ages were taken from the women's public social media profiles, and some were estimated from other available public data in cases when the exact age wasn't accessible. Also, some quotes are paraphrased from conversations I've had with female friends, colleagues, and relatives over the years.

As a man writing on this subject, I am fully aware that I still have much to learn. But I also believe my male perspective can bring something important to the conversation, simultaneously helping men recognize how our collective actions, attitudes, and blind spots are being passed down to our sons and also helping women learn about the male thought process to better understand their husbands, their sons, and the other men in their lives.

Much of men's collective disrespect has been unintentional, which is not an excuse, but it's an important factor. In my research and interviews with women for this project, one woman said, "Most men show some form of disrespect to women, but I'm convinced that it's usually unintentional. I believe most men would change if they recognized what they were saying or doing is being perceived by women as disrespectful."

I am on a journey of finding those blind spots in my own life and making sure I am doing all I can do to help my sons not repeat my mistakes. I'm working to reimagine my own role in this story and help other men (and women) do the same. For those of us who are parents (or stepparents), raising boys who respect girls represents one of our most sacred duties as dads or moms. Together, we can make lasting change by bringing more respect into the world.

I may not have been the most likely candidate to write this book, but I'm passionate about living out this message in my own life and with my own family. I'm on this journey myself, and I'm inviting you to join me. At the core I'm an encourager, and I want to leverage every bit of influence I can muster to encourage my generation to make positive changes to benefit the next generation.

I'm also a husband and the dad of four precious boys. My primary motivation in writing this book is to fulfill my sacred duty to teach them to respect their mom, respect the women they'll grow up to marry, to respect their future daughters, and to respect all the females in their lives. This might raise a question: "What about teaching girls to respect boys or teaching boys to respect other boys and respect themselves? Doesn't that matter too?"

Of course, I want my boys to respect males and respect themselves too—and that will be part of the discussion—but they (like most of us) have already been subconsciously and overtly conditioned to give respect to men more naturally than to women. Giving more respect to women won't diminish the amount of respect they give to men or to themselves. True respect never subtracts or divides; it multiplies. As for a book on teaching daughters what they should do, I'll leave that to someone who actually has daughters.

This book will address challenges and solutions that impact the entire globe, but these changes must be implemented one family at a time. I'm starting with my own. If my boys are the only ones impacted by the message of this book, it was well worth the effort in writing it. Of course, I hope you and your family are impacted as well. If even one person will embrace this message, the generational and relational impact will be immeasurable. If many of us will embrace and embody this message, the world will look different (and better) a generation from now!

Thank you for taking this journey with me. Thank you for being part of the solution to one of the world's most troubling problems. Thank you for taking a stand for all our sons and daughters. Let's get started.

CHAPTER 1

THE CURRENT CRISIS

Of all the evils for which man has made himself responsible, none is so degrading, so shocking or so brutal as his abuse of the better half of humanity; the female sex.

—MAHATMA GANDHI

The girls were screaming for help, but no one seemed to care. They were just poor orphaned teenagers, after all. Worthless. Troublemakers. Dirty. Disposable. Those were the labels they had been given by their supposed caretakers.

Those, of course, weren't accurate labels. The girls were actually so much more. Priceless. Beloved. Cherished. Chosen. Adopted. Those are the labels God had chosen for them, but the corrupt criminals running the orphanage seemed to care little what God might say.

The very people who should have been protecting these precious girls had been prostituting them. Forty teenage girls in a government-run orphanage were being abused, raped, and pimped out on a daily basis. As sickening and unimaginable as that was, it wasn't even the most shocking part of the story. These girls were about to burn to death while screaming for help.

This isn't the plot of a horror movie. This isn't something that happened hundreds of years ago. This happened in 2017 in a place I've been to often. The flight there from Atlanta is a shorter one than flying from Atlanta to Los Angeles.

The details of this story are horrifying, grisly, and evil: forty teenage girls systematically raped while under the care of the government and then left to die in a gruesome fire. You'd think it would have been the main news story around the clock for months straight, but chances are you've never heard of it until now. In fact, other than a series of articles run by the *New York Times*, few major media outlets in the United States even covered the story.[1]

When I learned about these precious girls being treated as disposable commodities, I was disgusted, shocked, outraged, and heartbroken. It was a moment of personal awakening for me, and I knew I had to do more to be part of the solution. I wanted to be part of protecting the next generation of women in my own neighborhood and around the world.

This tragedy took place in Guatemala, and it hit close to home for me. I've traveled there frequently with a group from church, because we support a Christian orphanage there called Casa Shalom. There's an orphan crisis in Guatemala, which has been complicated by a long civil war, murders fueled by violent drug cartels, and the lack of a foster care system or outside adoptions. The orphans are many, and they have become defenseless prey to the repugnant, perverted human traffickers, pimps, and child abusers.

Just because this tragedy took place outside my nation's borders doesn't mean I should be any less outraged than if it had happened next door. God has called us to a faith without borders. It was Dr. Martin Luther King Jr. who poignantly declared, "A threat to justice anywhere is a threat to justice everywhere." I'll paraphrase Dr. King by surmising that "disrespect to women anywhere is disrespect to women everywhere."

We all need to become aware of the current crisis impacting women in our own communities, but we need a more comprehensive global awareness as well. Orphanages like Casa Shalom are doing world-changing work for the vulnerable children in their care. Many of their kids have experienced horrific abuse, but the staff at the orphanage shows those kids the love of Jesus, which is more powerful than all the brokenness in the world. It's a wonderful, life-giving place where children are able to heal from the deepest of wounds and rediscover the simple joys of childhood once more. Casa Shalom is a place where kids feel loved and safe, and because of that, they're able to become kids again.

I've laughed at Casa Shalom, and I've cried there. I've heard heartbreaking stories, and I've heard beautiful, inspiring ones. I've been beaten badly at soccer by the boys. I've giggled with the girls as I've tried to communicate through my gringo Spanish. I've sat on the mountainside and enjoyed the sunset over a distant volcanic mountain while watching these precious kids laugh and play and sing at one of the most beautiful places I've ever seen. It seems to be a place where heaven and earth meet and kiss each other.

My visits to Casa Shalom caused me to fall in love not only with the kids at the orphanage but with the beautiful country of Guatemala as a whole and the beautiful people within it. Unfortunately, not all the orphanages are as safe and loving as Casa Shalom. Some of the government-run facilities have become cesspools of corruption and abuse, as the tragic fire brought to light. When I heard about those forty girls who died, I immediately pictured the names and faces of the girls at Casa Shalom who came from similar circumstances. My heart broke.

I'm not sharing this story at the start of the book to set a melodramatic tone. I'm not trying to paint a bleak or hopeless picture when it comes to the current state of affairs. On the contrary, I want us to take action and live out a faith without borders to bring healing, hope, and respect to women and girls around the world. I want us to empower our sons to be part of the solution on a global scale.

You and I are standing at a significant crossroads. We have an unprecedented opportunity within our reach. This opportunity represents a chance to right a wrong that has existed across cultures worldwide since the dawn of human history. It can end with our generation and give birth to a new era, impacting and improving nearly every aspect of life on earth.

I know what you're probably thinking. *That was the most melodramatic paragraph I've ever read in my life!*

Just to own the awkwardness, I'd be skeptical, too, if I read a paragraph like that. I would assume somebody was getting ready to sell me an overpriced timeshare or convince me to switch religions to help them meet their door-to-door monthly convert quota. We've been conditioned to be skeptical whenever we see exaggerated language, because it's usually a tool of marketers or politicians using hyperbole to try and move us to action, but their overhyped words never seem to match up with reality.

I firmly believe the situation outlined in this book is something different. First, I'm not a marketer or a politician. I'm not asking for your vote, and I'm not asking you to buy anything (except for purchasing this book, and I'm assuming you've already purchased it, which I appreciate because I have four sons to put through college). The opportunity I'm referencing is something that doesn't directly benefit me beyond the collective benefit of living in a world where this problem is corrected.

So, I'll get straight to the point. The opportunity before us is realizing we have the potential, for the first time in human history, of creating a world where girls and women can experience equal respect and equal opportunity from their male counterparts and from the cultural systems at large. I'm not just talking about preventing future orphanage fires (although that's obviously important too). I'm talking about changing the entire climate of disrespect toward women and girls, which has existed in various forms since the dawn of human civilization.

The tide of change has been building, and now we're at a defining crossroads. We all have an important role to play to make sure the next generation is the first to experience equality of respect and opportunity, and one of the vital keys in this equation is parents raising boys who respect girls.

This might sound like an overly simplistic approach to an incredibly complex issue, but the approach I'm proposing isn't nearly as simplistic as it might seem on the surface. It will challenge our deeply held assumptions, common misinterpretations of Scripture, and invisible biases that have lived in our blind spots for a lifetime. If we're willing to take this journey, it could transform our hearts, our homes, and our spheres of influence. If enough of us will do this together, we have the potential to change the world. Seriously.

THE WAKE-UP CALL

Love and respect women. Look to her not only for comfort, but for strength and inspiration and the doubling of your intellectual and moral powers. Blot out from your mind any idea of superiority; you have none.

—GIUSEPPE MAZZINI

Our current reality marks a unique time in history. We've experienced a collective wake-up call as it relates to sexism. I've been as shocked and disheartened as anyone else as I've watched the news and learned that some of my biggest childhood heroes have turned out to be serial rapists. In the aftershocks of the #MeToo movement, revelations and accusations keep coming in. Revered men in entertainment, politics, ministry, business, and all other walks of life have been exposed as sexual harassers, misogynists, and serial womanizers.

My four sons are growing up in this climate. They watch the news. They see stories and chatter online. They come to me with questions, and I desperately want to get this right. I want to provide the tools, the answers, and the examples they'll need to be self-respecting men who are also fiercely respectful of women. If I raise sons who are outwardly successful in every way imaginable but disrespectful to women, then I will have failed as a father.

Raising boys who respect girls is a mission I share with my incredible wife, Ashley. As she and I watched the news together recently as yet another story broke, I felt a righteous anger welling up inside of me. Ashley said out loud what my heart was feeling. She poignantly declared, "As a mom, I can't think of anything more heartbreaking than the thought of our boys growing up and being abusive to women or using women or being vulgar with women."

Her words were like a lightning rod of truth for me, and it brought clarity to an area where I'd previously only felt anger and frustration. Like the orphanage fire, Ashley's declaration became a milestone moment in this journey. Now, when I see these tragic stories on the news or hear details of another girl or woman being abused, mistreated, or disrespected, instead of feeling only anger or despair, I feel motivation to be part of the change.

As parents, we can help the next generation of men know how to respect, protect, and champion the next generation of women. We must. Anything less is unacceptable. The cycle of mistreatment can and should end once and for all with our generation. I want my boys to grow up to be protectors and respecters of women. I want them to do everything in their power to create a world where all women and girls feel safe, so I need to do everything in my power as a parent to equip them with the right tools and truths.

I'd like to think that our world is heading in the right direction. On the surface, there's been much progress for females worldwide. There's certainly some good news in this ongoing narrative, but in many ways, the situation is more discouraging than it's ever been.

> AS PARENTS, WE CAN HELP THE NEXT GENERATION OF MEN KNOW HOW TO RESPECT, PROTECT, AND CHAMPION THE NEXT GENERATION OF WOMEN.

This book is going to have many moments that are uplifting and inspiring. There will even be plenty of humor and lighthearted fun, but here at the start, we need to get straight to the bad news. I'll expound further on some of the following sobering statistics throughout the book, but for now, we need to look at a realistic snapshot of the crisis we're facing so that we can more clearly walk forward:

- Violence toward women and the slavery of women (primarily through human trafficking of domestic workers and sex slaves) is at an all-time high. There has never been a time in world history when more women were enslaved than right now. More than 70 percent of all modern-day slaves are females.[2]

- Many of the girls trapped in sexual slavery are between the ages of nine and seventeen. These underaged girls are often kidnapped, beaten, and abused by pimps and then forced to perform sex acts on up to sixty men per day just to be allowed to eat or sleep.[3]

- One of the leading causes of death among women aged sixteen to forty-five is homicide by their husband or boyfriend. Men are killed by women at only one-tenth that rate. In dating relationships men's greatest fear is usually rejection, while women fear for their physical safety or even their lives.[4]

- Approximately 70 percent of female sexual abuse victims never report their abuse for fear of not being believed.[5]

- In recent survey research, 30 percent of college men who identified themselves as respecters of women also admitted they would be willing to rape a woman if they knew they wouldn't be caught.[6]

- More than $17 million of taxpayer money has gone to settle sexual harassment suits against male members of the United States Congress who have sexually harassed female staff members.[7]

- More than 200 million women and girls worldwide have been victims of female genital mutilation, which is a horrendous and painful assault on girls' genitals to surgically remove or alter the clitoris and/or vagina, numbing sexual sensation. This barbaric, misogynistic practice is designed to keep females sexually pure and subservient to their husbands. The torturous ritual is often performed by someone with no medical training in filthy environments. Many girls have died from botched procedures.[8]

- One-third of girls in the developing world are married before the age of eighteen. One in nine are married before the age of fifteen. Many of these marriages are forced marriages to much older men, and they are often polygamous.[9]
- At least one in five women will be the victim of a sexual assault in her lifetime, and more than 50 percent of women will be victims of some form of sexual harassment.[10]
- Women are victims of physical violence in domestic abuse situations at a rate nearly ten times higher than men are victimized.[11]
- Seventy percent of teen boys and men view pornography with some regularity, and nearly half of all teenage boys and men show signs of addiction to porn. The porn addiction crisis is creating massive negative repercussions, as I'll discuss in a later chapter.[12]
- In both school and work settings, women and girls are more likely than men to be interrupted. They are also more likely to be given a disproportionate amount of the workload in group projects. They are also paid less on average than their male counterparts.[13]
- The average child is exposed to approximately fourteen

thousand sexual references via television per year. Sexual references on TV and advertising depict nudity or partial nudity in women nearly ten times as often as men are shown nude or partially nude.[14]

- One hundred percent of our sons will grow up to either become part of the problem or part of the solution.

- One hundred percent of parents are responsible for making sure these stats look different a generation from now. It begins with how we live our own lives, and how we teach our children.

As shocking as these statistics are, they don't tell the whole story. There's no stat to capture the icky feeling a young woman experiences when she becomes the object of a man's unwanted gawking. There's no stat to measure the violation a woman feels when her social media selfie gets rated 1 to 10 or captioned with sexual innuendos by creepers on the other side of a smartphone screen. There are no stats to measure the men who surreptitiously objectify or mistreat women in subtle ways while maintaining a reputation as respecters of women.

These stats also don't tell the countless stories of the individuals and institutions that outwardly champion women while secretly mistreating or abusing them. One of the most shocking news stories of the past few years exposed the supposed women's empowerment organization NXIVM (pronounced "Nexium"), which lured young women under the guise of empowerment but then manipulated and molested them. The victims of this sexist cult were primarily affluent, intelligent, and highly educated women. The male leader of this organization was publicly a vocal supporter of women, but he secretly used his cult-like organization and influence to build a harem of personal sex slaves, even having some of the women branded with his initials displaying his "ownership" over them.[15] The example of NXIVM is an extreme case, but there are many other stories that will never make the news: stories of presumably respectful men abusing their positions of power to mistreat women.

I don't want to raise my sons to one day contribute to these horrific statistics, stories, and practices. I don't want them to become another example of the shameful behaviors we have seen from so many leaders and celebrities. I don't want my boys to become men who are respectful to women on the surface, but then harbor a dark side where these kinds of sinister and sexist behaviors can lurk. I don't want them to have an outward respect concealing an inward, insidious vulgarity toward women.

I want my sons to be men of integrity. I want them to be respecters of women. I want them to be men worthy of a future wife's respect. I want to be part of a generation of parents who are raising boys who respect girls. I'm assuming you want these same things for your children, and I applaud you for intentionally investing time and energy to be part of the solution. We as parents and educators have much more influence than we often assume.

As an important clarification before we go further, I want to reassure you that this book isn't about how men are bad and are completely responsible for the world's problems. This book isn't about male bashing or promoting any kind of political agenda. It's also not assuming men always have to be the heroes and rescuers and women are helpless victims. This book is simply a call to action to collectively right one of the greatest wrongs our world has ever known. Women and girls are being exploited and mistreated in various ways worldwide, and our children have the power to permanently correct these wrongs if we equip them.

REALITY MIGHT BE EVEN WORSE THAN THE STATISTICS

When I see all the bad stuff in the news that men have done to women, and when I see the way some of the boys in my school treat girls and talk about girls, it sometimes makes me embarrassed to be a boy.

—AIDEN B. (AGE 14)

It's easy to read through statistics like the ones I shared and almost gloss over their weight. To help ourselves feel better about the world in which we live, we have a mental predisposition to disregard negative statistics. We tell ourselves that it can't be as bad as the numbers suggest. All that bad news is just there to sell newspapers, right?

Sadly, in the case of sexual violence against women, there's evidence to suggest the stats are actually underreporting a vast amount of sexual crimes against women. Recently, there has been backlash in the news targeting victims of sexual assault who didn't report the crimes immediately. The news spin seems to suggest that if a woman doesn't immediately report, then the accusations must not be credible.

In direct response to those who would discredit the brave victims who reported their harrowing ordeals, countless people on Twitter showed solidarity by tweeting their own stories of unreported sexual abuse using the hashtag #WhyIDidntReport. The stories started trending and eventually become a viral news story featuring courageous confessions from students, soccer moms, scholars, and women from all walks of life. The voices included ministry leaders like Beth Moore, celebrities like actress Alyssa Milano, and Ronald Reagan's daughter, Patti Davis.

These short, tweet-length stories are heartbreaking, harrowing, eye-opening, sickening, and inspiring. I was deeply moved as I read through hundreds of these accounts. As we consider the reality of our current situation, let's consider what so many have faced and the circumstances that led to their silence.[16]

- "I was 16. I lied about where I was that night. I was drinking underage. I had had sex before. A defense attorney would try to make me look like a lying promiscuous teen w/ no regard for the law or my parents. I didn't know I'd still be trying to heal 23 yrs later."[17]
- "Because I was sexually abused at such a young age I didn't even know it was a crime. I didn't have the language to say what was happening to me. Later, as a teen, the sexual harassment and coercion of girls & women was seen the norm, not something to report."[18]
- "When I was 17, during the summer after I graduated

High School, I was supposed to be on a date and ended up the guy took me to a house and 5 guys raped me. I am 72 years old now and this is the first time I have ever spoken up. I have been too ashamed to report."[19]

- "I was molested at 8 by a school janitor, frightened to silence, gang raped at 18 by 2 boys at a party, I had been drinking and blamed myself, I felt shame. My parents never knew. I told my daughters 5 years ago, when I was 60. It took courage to tell even then."[20]

- "'The CDC estimates that over 1 million women are raped each year and only 3% of perpetrators are brought to justice,' CEO of @YMCABrooklyn."[21]

There are many thousands more like the ones I just shared, but hopefully this small sampling paints a picture of the hidden pain countless women are carrying. I also hope these stats and stories move us to action. It's not enough just to empathize or to feel badly for victims; we must rise up and declare, "No more!" We must make sure our sons understand the gravity of their choices. We must remember that these stats and stories represent real women whose lives have been irrevocably wounded by the selfish sexual aggression of misguided men.

THE REAL PEOPLE BEHIND STATS AND STORIES

Perhaps one of the reasons there's been inaction or apathy around the startling stats is simply because we only view them as stats. We don't view these numbers as representing real women with names and faces. Even when we do identify a female victim by name, we often unintentionally suggest that her value is only tied to her relationship to a man. How many times have you heard said of a female victim of violence or disrespect: "What a terrible crime! She's somebody's daughter. She's somebody's sister. She's somebody's mother."

Of course, our relational connections are a vital part of our humanity, but our good intentions also reveal a double standard. We rarely refer to male victims with the same language. When we fall into double standards like this, we're showing a form of disrespect. We're basing a woman's worth on her relationships to men instead of the fact that she's an eternal soul bearing the image of God and carrying limitless worth equal to any man.

I might be splitting hairs or getting too legalistic on soapboxes in the example I just gave, but I want to be aware of my own blind spots. The process of researching and writing this book has been a painful one, because I've had to face many aspects of my own hypocrisy and blindness in these areas. I've been smacked in the face with the reality of some of the misguided mind-sets I've had. I'll even be sharing some embarrassingly intimate details of my own journey in the chapters ahead.

If you are going to get the full benefit of this journey, and if you want your sons to fully grasp these truths, there will likely be uncomfortable moments along the way. When things start feeling awkward or uncomfortable, please have the courage to stick with it. I promise the end result will be well worth the struggles. In any part of life, great breakthroughs are preceded by great barriers.

Throughout the journey that led to this book, there were many uncomfortable moments that tempted me to walk away. Some stories were so unnerving and shocking that the thought of diving deeper into them overwhelmed me. One of those stories ultimately became a catalyst, putting a fire inside me to see this project to completion. It started on a road trip, listening to a podcast.

ANOTHER GIRL IN ANOTHER FIRE

Ashley and I spend a lot of time in the car, because we travel to speak as part of our marriage ministry and we also make family trips to visit our out-of-state relatives. One of our road-trip traditions has been to find a good podcast to help pass the time. Our favorites tend to be unfolding stories about unsolved mysteries. On our last road trip we discovered the wildly popular podcast *Up and Vanished*. The podcast's first season chronicled the cold case of a missing young woman in Georgia named Tara Grinstead.[22]

It instantly pulled us in, because it took place in Georgia. We lived in Georgia for a decade, and the familiar Southern drawls of the townsfolk being interviewed were like a warm, nostalgic trip down memory lane. The story itself was also captivating. By the end of the first episode, we were already hooked and desperate to find out exactly what happened to Tara.

RAISING BOYS WHO RESPECT GIRLS

To summarize the backstory, Tara Grinstead was a school-teacher and former beauty queen in her late twenties. She lived in a small town about an hour south of Atlanta. She had competed in the Miss Georgia pageant in her early twenties and then became an educator and pageant coordinator, helping and mentoring young girls. She was a kindhearted, compassionate, and committed teacher and a vibrant part of the community. Everybody seemed to love and respect her.

On a Saturday that started off like any other, Tara went to a beauty pageant to support the girls she was mentoring. After the pageant ended, she drove to a cookout hosted by her school's principal and spent time watching college football and hanging out with coworkers. She left the cookout and headed home. When she didn't show up for her class on Monday morning, her absence alarmed the school administrators. The police were sent to her home.

They found Tara's car, keys, and cell phone at her house, but there was no sign of Tara. An investigation was immediately launched, and search parties began to scour the area, but she had truly up and vanished.

With each episode of the podcast, the investigators interviewed people who knew Tara and reexamined old clues. While the podcast was unfolding in real time with weekly episodes, a break was made in the case. Ashley and I looked at each other in shock when episode twelve of the podcast started with breaking news that an arrest had just been made. I was practically holding my breath when the recording of the Georgia Bureau of Investigation press conference started and Tara's family made a statement.

There are many important details in Tara's story that I won't elaborate on here, but I will get to the point of what happened and why I'm recording her story in this book. At the time of this writing, the trial of Tara's accused attackers has not taken place. What we know is that two former students were involved in her disappearance. There's still uncertainty around the motive of her murder, but what we know for certain is that Tara was killed and her body was burned to cover up the evidence.

The two young men who burned Tara's body were part of a larger group of friends who often gathered in that area for bonfire parties. Evidence suggests that these other friends knew about the entire cover-up and may have even been at the bonfire when Tara's body was burned. This group kept the secret for years until a break was made in the case and the truth began to unravel.

I listened to almost twenty hours of the podcast, and by the end of it, I felt like I knew Tara. I felt invested in the process, and I pray she gets justice for the unspeakable crimes committed against her. I still get sick to my stomach thinking about what she went through.

One of the most disturbing aspects of this entire case was the almost flippant nature of the men involved, who callously burned her body and then moved on with their lives. One was the son of a prominent Georgia politician, and it seemed that this young man valued his family's reputation far more than he valued Tara's life.

Tara was burned as though she was trash. She was used and treated like a disposable commodity. She was naked when they burned her, which only added to the objectification and disrespect inherent in this horrific crime. They stripped her of all power and they stripped her of all clothing, but their disrespect couldn't strip her of her humanity. It was their own humanity they sacrificed in those flames.

I kept wondering how anyone could be as coldhearted and calloused as this group of friends must have been to participate in such a crime. Even now, I keep wondering why and how they could keep a secret like that. How could they watch Tara's family stricken by grief and desperate for answers? How could they go on drinking beer together and hanging out, acting as if it had never happened? How much disrespect for women could they possibly possess to carry out this crime and then keep it a secret?

I refuse to live in a world where women are burned like trash. These examples may be extreme and rare, but the sexist mentality that led to these vicious crimes is widespread. There is something broken within the heart of mankind to allow these broken mind-sets to persist. I want to do my part to put an end to stories like this one.

Women deserve better. Men deserve better as well. Both men and women lose when half the human race is objectified, mistreated, and devalued simply because of their gender. We must collectively rise up and do more. We must teach our sons a better way. We must create a safer world for our daughters.

Please don't let these negative stats and stories make you feel hopeless. I know it's been a somber start to this journey, but we need to know how dark the darkness really is before we can fully appreciate the light. The truth is that there is hope.

We have more power than we realize to make the needed changes. The rest of this book will explain how to take the first steps in the right direction.

I fall short many times— I'm not the perfect example my sons need—and you fall short as well. Despite our best efforts and our best intentions, we're not always the role models our kids need. Thankfully, there is one man who got it right. There's one our kids can look to as a perfect example, and we can look to him as well. When

> BOTH MEN AND WOMEN LOSE WHEN HALF THE HUMAN RACE IS OBJECTIFIED, MISTREATED, AND DEVALUED SIMPLY BECAUSE OF THEIR GENDER.

we're following in his example, we'll always be headed in the right direction. We'll learn exactly how in the next chapter.

In Women's Own Words

"Most men are good men. Most boys are good boys. A few rotten eggs give a bad name to the whole bunch, which isn't fair. Assume the best in men and you'll usually be right."

—INGRID K. (AGE 80)

"I feel respected when men make an effort to guard their heart not only with their eyes physically but when it comes to electronics, videos, and movies. Sexual purity is something taken so lightly by so many now—both men and women. I am very thankful for a husband who is very active in guarding his eyes."

—BONNIE D. (AGE 55)

"I feel most respected with gentle honesty. Also, being emotionally and physically protected in all situations."

—CHRISTI B. (AGE 28)

"The guys at my college are so hard to figure out. Sometimes they act like the biggest advocates for women and sometimes they act like the biggest users of women. . . . it's hard to trust them."

—JEWEL P. (AGE 19)

CHAPTER 2

JESUS, RESPECTER
OF WOMEN

*Jesus Christ raised women above the condition
of mere slaves, mere ministers to the passions
of man, raised them by His sympathy, to be
Ministers of God.*

—FLORENCE NIGHTINGALE

I am one of the fortunate few. I was blessed to be raised in a home with a loving father who simultaneously modeled the positive ideals of manhood and was completely devoted, respectful, and loving to my mother. I also have an extraordinary, loving mother who embodied the greatest strengths of femininity and is a woman worthy of anyone's respect. I'm so thankful for their positive, authentic example, but I'm also aware that having a great example isn't good enough when there's so much at stake. We need our compasses pointing toward true north and not just vaguely in the right direction.

Part of the problem with teaching the right lessons to our sons about respecting women is in finding the right role models for them to follow. These days so many of the men we once looked to as mentors and role models—people providing a standard of behavior and a lifestyle worth following—have turned out to be the last ones on earth we should be imitating. Even when we remove them from the mix, though, the truth is, we're all imperfect people, and nobody quite measures up.

We may not be living a double life or involved in a sordid sexual scandal, but we as parents still fall short of being perfect role models. I want to be, and I work hard at it, but I'm also painfully aware of my own shortcomings.

I was trying to corral my kids toward our minivan in a crowded parking lot earlier today, and with all of them headed in different directions, I shouted out, "If you're not following me, then you're headed in the wrong direction!" I laughed at myself after I said it, because while I'd like to think I'm always the perfect example for my sons, there are plenty of times when I blow it. There are plenty of times when I'm lost and headed in the wrong direction because of my own foolishness, my own pride, my own sin, or a myriad of other limitations. I want to be their perfect role model in this area of respecting women, but I fully realize that I fall short every day.

We all need a clear, consistent, and perfect standard to

which we can aspire. If we don't know where the bull's-eye is located, we're essentially just throwing darts in the dark, never sure if we're hitting or missing the mark until it's too late. But if nobody around us seems to measure up, whose example can we follow when even the best leaders stray off course?

The good news is that there *is* a clear and perfect role model worth following: one man who set the standard flawlessly. Throughout this book will be many stories and examples of mentors whom I believe can be trusted in this area, but I want to start off by highlighting the only man who is a perfect example. As the apostle Paul once said, "Follow me as I follow Christ."

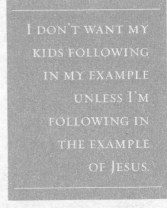

I DON'T WANT MY KIDS FOLLOWING IN MY EXAMPLE UNLESS I'M FOLLOWING IN THE EXAMPLE OF JESUS.

I don't want my kids following in my example unless I'm following in the example of Jesus. If we're following in the footsteps of Jesus, we'll always be headed in the right direction.

FOLLOWING JESUS' PERFECT EXAMPLE

Jesus is the only role model I've ever had who has never fallen short or let me down. As I said earlier, Jesus did more to elevate women than anyone else in history. He carried out his earthly ministry in a time when females were placed on the social hierarchy somewhere between animals and men, but Jesus elevated their status through his words, his actions, and his miracles. His countercultural approach to women was viewed as one of the most radical aspects of his ministry.

It's ironic that the very church Jesus started is now seen by many as an institution with repressive roots when it comes to respecting women. Both inside and outside the church, we need a history lesson about what Jesus actually did and what he actually taught. His timeless example is still our best example.

Let's travel back to the first-century Near East where Jesus lived and taught. Temporarily suspend your twenty-first-century mind-set for a moment, and try to connect with the folks living in Jesus' era. We need to understand the mind-set of the time, but we also need to understand the place. Let's start in Israel.

I had the privilege of traveling to Israel for the first time last year as part of a group of young influencers and peace-makers called the Israel Collective. It was a life-changing experience for me. The journey provided a colorful context for my study of the Bible. Before, the words were always in black and white, but when I read the Scriptures now, I see everything in three dimensions with vivid colors, sights, and sounds.

I can now see the places described. I know what it smells like in the Jerusalem markets. I've tasted some of the foods and wines Jews have been enjoying since the feasts and festivals recorded in the Old Testament. I've felt the sea breeze gently blowing around me as I watched the sun set over the Sea of Galilee. I've stood inside the empty Garden Tomb.

Travel there with me for a moment. Picture yourself high on the Mount of Beatitudes where Jesus preached the Sermon on the Mount. Imagine being in the crowd as Jesus first taught some of the most profound words ever spoken.

This carpenter-turned-rabbi didn't travel far in his lifetime. He didn't have the conveniences we take for granted. He never felt air conditioning. He never saw a television or a car or an airplane. His most advanced forms of travel were a small fishing boat or the back of a donkey. From the hilltop where he preached the sermon, he could look out and view the sea and villages where 90 percent of his life and ministry took place.

The wisdom he taught could not have come from his travels, because he hadn't really been anywhere. The wisdom couldn't have come from his parents, because they were simple, uneducated peasants. The wisdom couldn't have come from the Internet, because Siri and Google weren't around yet. No, this wisdom was from God alone.

He taught with authority. He taught with passion and with compassion. Nobody before or since has taught or lived like Jesus.

After Jesus listed out the famous Beatitudes, he told the crowd that they were the salt of the earth and that they were like a city on a hill. I picture him pointing to a hilltop in the distance where a city's light would have illuminated the sky. Jesus gave examples using the flowers and the birds, undoubtedly gesturing at his surroundings.

He used the world he created to help the people he created understand why they were created.

As the crowd was hanging on his every word, Jesus, the master teacher, abruptly and intentionally changed direction in his sermon. He began to quote the Old Testament laws, which would have been so familiar to his audience. But he wasn't just giving them a refresher course; he was changing their whole mind-set.

He told them that the law said not to commit murder, but now he was telling them that the law was the starting point, not the endgame. In fact, to even harbor anger toward someone was to commit murder in your mind and heart. Avoiding the deed might keep you out of prison, but you could still be locked up in a prison in your own heart. The law, Jesus revealed, wasn't just about behavior modification. It was there to be a form of training wheels for our hearts. It kept us inside the lines so we didn't wreck our lives, but its main purpose was to point us toward our need for a Savior who can bring real and lasting heart transformation. Our modified behavior and self-discipline never had the power to save us or change us, but Jesus had that power.

Next, Jesus, the great respecter of women, took this radical teaching to a place that was shocking. He reminded the audience that committing adultery was a sin, but now he was teaching that the true standard of purity and respect for women meant not even looking lustfully. He taught that what happens in our minds impacts our hearts and ultimately impacts our relationships.

Avoiding a physical affair was an important part of the equation, but Jesus brought the sobering truth that a sin that happens in our minds can be as damaging as a sin that happens in our bedrooms. Where our eyes go, our souls can follow.

Jesus was speaking to a crowd who didn't have the on-demand access to sexually charged images the way we do today. Most women were covered in loose-fitting garments and headscarves. There weren't Victoria's Secret ads on TV. There weren't swimming pools where you could look around and see women in bikinis. There weren't even yoga pants hugging the curves of a woman's hips. There certainly wasn't pornography, but still, there was lust.

Jesus was teaching the crowd, and teaching us, that women aren't to be viewed as objects to fulfill sinful sexual fantasies. God's daughters are to be viewed not as bodies to be used but as souls to be cherished and human beings to be respected. We can't say we respect women when we have an on-demand harem carrying out a mental orgy in our imaginations.

One of the most complicated dynamics in raising boys who respect girls is teaching boys that God created them to be visual and to be attracted to women's physical appearance, but, left unchecked, their visual appetites could warp their thinking and replace respect with objectification. This is one of the most important lessons we should be teaching our sons. It's also one of the most difficult for them to practice and is a lifelong struggle for most men. But Jesus, through his life, taught men how to respect women instead of lusting after them. I'd even argue that Jesus taught men how to look at women. Sure, we don't have photographs or videos showing how Jesus interacted with women, but the Gospels paint a vivid picture. In light of the historical context, we can see much about how Jesus must have looked at women. He looked at them with compassion, genuine concern, and grace.

Many women of Jesus' day had probably never been looked at in this way. What we know from historical context is that women were often viewed by men in one of three negative ways: with lust, with distrust, or with disgust. Let me briefly unpack each of these.

The "lust" part is pretty self-explanatory and something women in all cultures and all time periods have experienced. In Jesus' time, the Greek and Roman influences had brought in pagan practices, which normalized prostitution and even made having sex with temple prostitutes an act of worship. I suppose it was an effective outreach for men to say that they could come to worship and participate in an orgy with the female prostitutes, but it was not part of God's plan.

Jesus wanted to make it clear that God's plan for sex was specifically within the context of a monogamous, lifelong marriage. Later, the apostle Paul would take this teaching even further by reminding Christ-followers that to have sex is to become "one" with that person in a sacred way, and we should never become one with prostitutes. The very arrangement dehumanizes and disrespects all people involved and replaces love with lust.

Jesus' message was consistently about love, and the Bible consistently displays how love is the opposite of lust. Respect for women and lust of women can't coexist in the same mind. Each day, we must decide which one gets to stay.

The "distrust" view can be seen in how women's testimonies weren't considered valid in the courts of law in Jesus' day. There was a collective indifference and distrust toward the views, opinions, and even eyewitness accounts of women. Jesus turned this misogynistic, sexist viewpoint on its head in a variety of ways. He took the time to have many dialogues with women, some of whom most men would not have bothered to notice, much less have extended conversation with. The Gospels even report that it was women who first discovered his empty tomb.

The "disgust" viewpoint of Jesus' day was perhaps the most disrespectful mind-set of all. It forced women to the outskirts of society. It took regular parts of a woman's life, like her menstrual cycle, and stigmatized it. Blood flow made a person ceremonially unclean, meaning she couldn't participate in public worship or many other aspects of public life. For one week a month, a woman's menstrual cycle prohibited her from the most basic freedoms.

Jesus healed a woman who had suffered for twelve years with what the Bible describes as "an issue of blood." We don't know the exact circumstances, but the Scriptures infer she'd been afflicted with a severe form of endometriosis or a similar condition causing continuous blood flow and creating unimaginable physical, financial, emotional, and relationship hardships. With one touch, Jesus set her free from this ailment and all the stigmas that accompanied it.

There are countless other examples in the Gospels where Jesus showed his profound respect for women of all walks of life, from peasants and prostitutes to relatives and royalty. Some of his most touching tributes to womanhood can be found in his interactions with his mother, Mary.

Jesus' respect for his mother was a continuous theme throughout his life and ministry. His first miracle and his entrance into public ministry were propelled by an act of respect toward his mother, who requested that he help out a bride and groom about to face the social shame of running out of wine at their wedding. Jesus miraculously turned water to wine at his mother's urging.

One of Jesus' final acts before his death and resurrection was a touching tribute to his mother. He looked down from the cross into the eyes of his heartbroken mom, and then he looked at his friend and disciple John. He told Mary to look to John as a son, and he told John to care for Mary as he would his own mother. In their culture, family was the only real means of social support for widows, and Mary was widowed by the time of Jesus' crucifixion. Jesus wanted to make sure his mother was looked after. He clearly loved her and respected her.

Renowned theologian Dr. Wayne Grudem may have summed it up best in his book *Evangelical Feminism and Biblical Truth*. Dr. Grudem meticulously interprets Scripture and weighs his findings against the works of other biblical scholars and the shifting tides of public opinion. Dr. Grudem's research convinced him that Jesus never lowered men or men's unique biblical mandate to be servant leaders. He elevated men. But, just as importantly, Jesus elevated women too. Dr. Grudem explains,

> The overall picture, however, is that Jesus treated women as equals in a way that was surprising for first-century culture. We should be thankful that Jesus honored women, and treated them as persons just as He treated men. He talked openly with women, to the amazement of His disciples (John 4:1–27), taught women (Luke 10:38–42; John 4:7–26; 11:21–27), had women among the band of

disciples who traveled with Him (Luke 8:1–3), accepted monetary support and ministry from them (Mark 15:40–41; Luke 8:3), and used women as well as men as teaching examples (Mark 12:41–44; Luke 15:8–10; 18:1–8). Jesus thus set a pattern that should forever challenge all cultures that treat women as second-class citizens, as it no doubt challenged and rebuked the culture of Jesus' day.[1]

THE GOSPELS ARE A ROAD MAP FOR RESPECTING WOMEN

In all the written works of literature, science, and religion, there have never been documents that have brought more freedom and honor to women than the Gospels of Jesus Christ. The four biblical books of Matthew, Mark, Luke, and John are known as the Gospels, which is a term that simply means "good news." These four books record the life and teachings of Jesus, and they embody good news for all mankind—and for women in particular.

Starting with the very first lines of the very first Gospel, Matthew begins with the family lineage of Jesus. The reader can tell right away that this won't be a traditional story, because the lineage itself is anything but traditional. In the ancient cultures reading these original manuscripts, genealogies listed men only. It was as if women played no part in the story and contributed no genetics to the offspring.

These were cultures where women were expected to be silent, but from the beginning of the story of Jesus, women were given a voice and a place of honor. Through the lists of names and generations, Matthew broke from the traditional listing of fathers and began to highlight some mothers. He even highlighted mothers who had a scandalous past, like Rahab, who had been a prostitute before coming to faith in God.

Before the birth of Jesus had even been announced in Scripture, Jesus' life and ministry were put into the context of female heroes. The world might have defined women like Rahab in terms of sex or sin, but God defined them by their faith and chose to use these remarkable heroines to be an honorable part of the foundation on which Jesus would build his kingdom. From Rahab the ancestor of Jesus to Mary the mother of Jesus, the earliest heroes of the Gospels included women.

Women were heroes at the beginning of the Gospels, but they were also some of the most prominent heroes at the end. When all Jesus' male disciples abandoned him as he hung on the cross, it was Jesus' mother, Mary, and Jesus' friend Mary Magdalene who faithfully and courageously stood by. When the empty tomb was discovered, again women were there first. The Gospels are the story of Jesus, but it's impossible to tell the story of Jesus without simultaneously celebrating the story of women.

Women weren't only present at the beginning and the end of

> THE GOSPELS ARE THE STORY OF JESUS, BUT IT'S IMPOSSIBLE TO TELL THE STORY OF JESUS WITHOUT SIMULTANEOUSLY CELEBRATING THE STORY OF WOMEN.

the Gospels. On every page, Jesus' interactions with women are integral aspects of his overall story. Here are just a few of Jesus' many interactions with women:

- Jesus' longest-recorded one-on-one conversation was with a woman. (The woman at the well, John 4)
- Jesus raised Jairus's daughter from the dead. In all the recorded examples of Jesus raising someone from the dead, this little girl is the only person Jesus took by the hand. (Luke 8:50–56)
- Jesus healed Peter's mother-in-law. (Matt. 8:14–15)
- Jesus healed a woman who had suffered with a bleeding condition that had ostracized her from society for many years. (Mark 5:25–34)
- Two of Jesus' closest friends were sisters named Mary and Martha. (Luke 10:38–42)
- Jesus stood up for a woman who had been caught in adultery, and he ultimately saved her from death by a public stoning. (John 8:1–11)
- Jesus heard the pleas of a desperate widow whose only son had died, and he raised the son back to life. (Luke 7:11–17)
- Jesus healed a paralytic woman. (Luke 13:10–17)
- Jesus praised an impoverished widow for her generosity and elevated her as the standard of giving to which we should all aspire. (Luke 21:1–4)
- Jesus praised the persistence of a widow and described her as a model of the faith and persistence we should have when praying to God. (Luke 18:1–8)

There are many other examples of Jesus elevating the dignity of women in countercultural ways. Dignity and respect for women was clearly a cornerstone of his life and ministry. Those of us who consider ourselves followers of Christ should be on the forefront of this ongoing struggle to bring respect and opportunities to women and girls worldwide. It's not enough to simply believe Jesus' teachings; we must be willing to take a stand by putting our faith into action.

FOLLOWING JESUS' EXAMPLE OFTEN REQUIRES TAKING A STAND

Beth Moore is a prominent Bible teacher and author who has shown great courage in this ongoing conversation about respecting women. Beth has always stayed away from politics, and despite a massive platform and her tremendous reputation within the evangelical world, she's been humble and even deferential to male leaders within the church. When a prominent politician was recorded saying some vulgar and crude comments about women, Beth was shocked by the tacit approval of church leaders who dismissed the vulgarity as just "locker room talk." She realized she had a moral responsibility to step into this controversial dialogue.

In an uncharacteristic foray into the political debate on Twitter, Beth Moore courageously called out the Christians who excused sexist, objectifying language. In blunt terms, she began sharing some of the sexism and vulgarity she and other women have experienced within the church. She called

Christian men back to the standard of dignity, equality, and respect for women that Jesus himself set for us.

She was willing to step into the controversy for the sake of bringing hope and help to the many women who have suffered in silence under the manipulation and control of powerful and morally compromised men. She risked her own platform to give a platform to victims who felt powerless. Her courage and candor on these issues have sparked healthy dialogues within the church and even in the secular media.[2]

I've always been inspired by people who display the courage to put their faith and their convictions into action even when it costs them dearly. Many of the great movements of history to bring justice and freedom to others have been sparked by followers of Christ who were simply asking themselves what Jesus would do in the same situation. For those of us who consider ourselves to be followers of Jesus, we have a unique opportunity and responsibility to lead the charge in bringing more respect and protection to women. We can learn much from modern heroes like Beth Moore, but we can also learn from the example of many brave and faith-filled heroes from the past.

There are many stories in history of unlikely heroes who have stepped into their moments of destiny to bring immeasurable impact and social change. Most of these people weren't looking for notoriety. They were simply willing to do the right thing when it mattered most. One such hero is a first-century monk named Telemachus.

Telemachus lived during the reign of the Roman Empire. During his lifetime Christianity was spreading rapidly, but the kingdom Christ preached seemed to conflict with the empire Rome was trying to build. Roman leaders were threatened by those who would follow a carpenter king with more loyalty than they'd follow Caesar.

It was a time of great violence and turmoil. Rome enforced their power with brutality, and any enemies or perceived enemies of the empire were killed in gruesome and public ways. The public executions and crucifixions were meant to be a deterrent to those who would challenge Roman rule and supremacy. The most famous example of gratuitous violence and death took place in the Roman Colosseum, where gladiators would fight to the death for the entertainment of the masses.

The gladiator games fed the bloodlust of the people. Otherwise mild-mannered citizens would become drunk on the violence and spectacle. The Colosseum was packed daily with people watching prisoners and persecuted Christians being chased and eaten alive by hungry lions, or gladiators fighting to the death. Some gladiators were considered to be professional athletes, but most of them were prisoners who were forced to fight to the death in the hopes of one day earning their freedom.

This was a sick game with no winners. Those who performed in the arena never truly won, because they were essentially slaves to a broken system from which they could rarely escape. The spectators never won, because even though they felt entertained by the momentary thrill of the battle, the dehumanizing violence almost certainly had a negative impact on their daily lives and experiences.

At the height of the gladiator games' popularity, an unassuming Christian monk named Telemachus was making his first visit to the big city of Rome. He wasn't sure what to expect, because he hailed from a rural setting. His life had been a simple one of prayer and of service to others, but he felt compelled by God to visit the busy metropolis of Rome.

Telemachus stepped off the boat in the Roman port, and I would bet his eyes widened as he processed all the sights, sounds, and smells of the big city. He'd never seen anything like it before. As he tried to get his bearings, he quickly found himself being swept up into the current of a moving crowd. Thousands of people were rushing into the Colosseum, and Telemachus followed the crowd into the huge stadium.

Not knowing what to expect, he looked around and saw raving fans screaming and clapping at the dusty ground at the center of the arena. Telemachus turned his eyes to the center of the stadium and was shocked to see men battling to the death. With every clang of the sword, with every spilling of blood and with every kill, the crowd became enraptured with enthusiasm. Telemachus was shocked at the depravity and inhumanity he saw all around him.

The monk began trying to appeal to the people around him, but no one would listen to him. They were so engrossed in the battle. Telemachus realized the only way to bring any change would be to put himself on the field. Throwing caution to the wind, the monk rushed to the wall separating the seats from the field of battle and hurled himself over. He was now unarmed and completely vulnerable.

Telemachus began running to gladiators as they fought and pleading with them to stop. He fearlessly shouted, "In the name of the Lord Jesus Christ, King of Kings and Lord of Lords, I command these wicked games to cease. Do not requite God's mercy by shedding innocent blood."[3]

The gladiators probably assumed he was a drunk spectator, and they tossed him aside. Telemachus persisted, and his ubiquitous presence on the field of battle went from an entertaining sideshow to an annoying nuisance in the eyes of the spectators. In their lust for more blood, the spectators began shouting, "Kill him! Kill him!"

Fueled by public pressure, one of the gladiators took his sword and ran it through the torso of the unarmed monk. Telemachus fell on his knees in the middle of the Colosseum. It was the place in the stadium where the acoustics were best, so for the first time, the entire crowd could hear what the man had been shouting all along. With his dying breaths, he shouted once more, "In the name of Christ, stop this!"

As Telemachus died in the center of that bloody arena, the cheering stopped, and a silence swept over the crowd. The gladiators stopped fighting, unsure what to do next. One by one, spectators began leaving the stadium in a solemn silence. Haunted and convinced by what they'd just seen, their collective conscience had been seared.

In one single act of courage, a simple man of faith turned the tide of public opinion on one of the most brutal (and popular) traditions of the ancient world. He also pointed the pagan crowd toward the hope that is found in Christ alone.

A generation later, Rome would be a very different place. The gladiator games had ended for good and Christianity had gone from a persecuted religion to the official religion of the empire. There were, of course, many factors at play to make these changes a reality, but I'm convinced the courage and self-sacrifice of Telemachus and other unsung heroes like him was a huge part of turning the tide.[4]

Modern-day equivalents of the gladiator games are pornography and the sexual objectification of women in entertainment. Like the gladiator games, our commercialized objectification of women is seen as a staple of modern culture. It gives a cheap and momentary rush to the consumer who cheers for more. It provides incredible amounts of money for those profiting from the dehumanizing spectacle. It enslaves the performers and desensitizes the entire culture.

Like Telemachus, we need to have the courage to step into battle and say, "In the name of Christ, stop this!"

We must be willing to stand against popular public opinion and stand against those who are profiting from the objectification of women. We must stand against the lusts in our own souls that would justify the continuing sins in the pursuit of our own entertainment and self-gratification.

Even if it means self-sacrifice, we must all be willing to say, "In the name of Christ, stop this! Stop mistreating women. Stop prostituting women as a form of entertainment. Stop justifying pornography. Stop disrespecting women. Stop using women. Stop abusing women. Stop manipulating women. Stop cheating women. Stop hurting women. Stop silencing women. In the name of Christ, stop!"

In Women's Own Words

"I'm a sex abuse survivor who was first abused by a youth pastor in my home church. I was so confused, because this man I respected so deeply preyed on my admiration for him. That pastor was later prosecuted and the whole experience rocked my faith. I left the church and abandoned my faith for several years. After counseling and a long period of soul-searching, I've come back to God. I'm married to a wonderful Christian man. I've found healing and freedom from those past wounds, and I'm closer to Christ than I've ever been before, but I'll also say that anyone who uses a position of power in the church to prey on kids should spend their lives in prison."

—NORA P. (AGE 42)

"The most respectful treatment I've ever received has come from Christian men. Unfortunately, the most disrespectful treatment I've ever received has also come from Christian men."

—HANNAH T. (AGE 51)

"I go to a Christian college, and there are so many guys here who are trying to treat girls the right way. There are so many guys in accountability groups with other guys to stay sexually pure and stay away from porn. Even when they mess up, I believe most of the young men on campus really do love Jesus and they want to treat women the right way. A few bad examples always dominate the headlines, but nobody runs a

front-page story about all the good guys who are trying to live with integrity."

—CINDY K. (AGE 19)

"Jesus said that looking at a woman with lust is like committing adultery. Jesus always treated women as cherished souls and not as objects of lust. I'll bet Jesus always looked women in the eyes instead of looking down at them or looking at their bodies. If men would just follow Jesus' standard, porn would disappear and disrespect in all its forms would disappear. We need to bring back those old WWJD bracelets and actually ask ourselves, 'What would Jesus do?' Because what Jesus would do would be to always respect women."

—EMMA A. (AGE 35)

CHAPTER 3

THE LOCKER ROOM MENTALITY

*Boys laugh at what they put girls through, but
they won't be laughing when they wipe tears
off their daughter's face for the same reason.*

—WILL SMITH

A decade ago, I was working at a large, multisite church
in Florida. It was a vibrant, growing church, but one of
the youth pastors was hiding a sinister secret. This pastor was,
on the surface, a pillar of our community. His social media
posts and public persona painted the picture of a rock-solid
family man who adored his wife and kids and faithfully lived

out the message he preached to his youth group. But his carefully crafted reputation came crashing down the day he was arrested for having a yearlong sexual affair with a fifteen-year-old girl in his youth group.

I remember watching the news story of his arrest. He had been such a revered and dignified leader, but his mug shot depicted a distraught and humiliated hypocrite. He had broken the hearts of his wife and children. He had caused immeasurable damage to the church he had professed to love. He had shattered the innocence of a young girl and wounded her with lifelong emotional scars. Our community was left wondering how a man who had appeared to be so trustworthy, faithful, and respectable could be capable of such heinous acts.

He later confessed that he had harbored fantasies about this girl and others in his youth group but had wrongly assumed that his fantasies were harmless. He never believed he would act on them. He was disciplined in other areas of his life, so he had a prideful and misguided view of his own personal strength and restraint. He believed he was a good person and even a good pastor. In his mind, his fantasies were just a natural way to blow off steam and add some excitement to his predictable routine of work, bills, kids, and life in suburbia.

He had compartmentalized part of his mind where his dark fantasies could live, but sinful fantasies never stay in the tidy compartments we try to keep them in. As he would later confess, the first time he had sexual contact with this girl, it happened so effortlessly because he had replayed this scenario in his mind a thousand times. He had systematically desensitized himself and removed the moral compass that had guided him all his life.

I'm sure he never imagined he would be committing statutory rape in the sound booth of a sanctuary after a youth worship service, but on an otherwise uneventful Wednesday night, that's exactly what happened. Whatever thoughts we allow to replay in our minds will eventually shape our actions. In an instant, his "harmless" fantasies had given birth to unimaginable consequences for himself, for his victim, and for countless others.

Tragically, I've spoken to many women over the years who have been similarly abused by men in positions of authority. I've heard heartbreaking tales of harassment, exploitation, and assault at the hands of men once trusted and admired. This list of abusers and womanizers includes preachers, bosses, educators, relatives, politicians, mentors, and a myriad of other categories. These men have misused their influence, selfishly defiling and disregarding women and girls as if they were nothing more than disposable objects in a game of sexual conquest.

One of the common trends among these predatory men is the ability to keep up a respectable public persona while living a secret life of sexual deviance. In their arrogance, they seem to believe that their actions are consequence-free, but there is always a high cost to a double life. We can't compartmentalize our lives and believe that what we do in secret won't eventually come out. Another way to say "compartmentalize" is "compartmental lies." Those lies will catch up with us. They always do.

Scripture gives us the sobering warning that everything done in secret will eventually be shouted from rooftops, and what is done in the darkness will always be illuminated eventually. And all along the way, the damage done by our choices will continue to build. The consequences for sexual sin create repercussions not only for those directly involved but for many others who become collateral damage in the aftermath. Temporary pleasure is never worth the permanent regrets.

> TEMPORARY PLEASURE IS NEVER WORTH THE PERMANENT REGRETS.

Perhaps the greatest tragedy in this entire situation with my former colleague is that all the pain and devastation was completely preventable. It never had to happen. It never should have happened. I'm sure he would give anything to travel back in time and undo the damage his reckless actions caused, the ripple effect that has spread throughout an entire community. As he sits alone in a prison cell, I'm sure he's haunted by the pain his family and his young victim are feeling.

Like me, you probably feel anger toward the perpetrator in this story. I believe we should feel a righteous anger and desire for justice when women and girls are mistreated and abused. While we should feel a righteous anger toward the criminals and compassion for the victims, I also believe we should feel a third emotion. We should feel terror. I don't mean to sound melodramatic here, but I believe we as parents of boys should be terrified by knowing that so many men who come from "good" families and who have "good" reputations in the community have turned out to be sexual predators.

There's a pervasive mind-set in our culture that has caused

so many decent men to commit horrifically indecent acts. A misguided mentality has taken root, and the consequences are devastating. As parents, we must not remain blind to these toxic mind-sets. We must not believe the lies that only monsters lurking in dark alleyways are capable of such depravity. We must face the sobering truth that any man is capable of falling into this deep pit of sin if his mind, his heart, his eyes, and his actions don't remain focused in the right direction.

As you reflect on the troubling details of this heartbreaking story from my former church, I'm sure you want to believe that your son is incapable of such horrific acts. I certainly want to think the same about my own sons. No parent wants to believe this dark path is possible, and no boy believes that someday he will grow up to bring shame on his family and cause great pain in the lives of others. And yet, many boys will tragically grow up to do exactly that.

We must teach our sons to live with integrity and avoid the pervasive pitfalls of living a double life. We must guide our sons to develop the right mind-set so they can approach relationships from a healthier place. We must help our sons to view women and girls as coheirs in God's family and not as commodities to be exploited. We must equip our sons to avoid the tendencies and temptations birthed from the toxic mind-set I call "the Locker Room Mentality."

"The boys on my eighth-grade basketball team talk about porn and sex the whole time we're in the locker room. One guy even showed the team a cell-phone video of his girl-friend giving him [oral sex]. Another guy has shown naked

pictures of girls he's hooked up with. There's always someone showing porn too. These same guys act so different
in public. My parents have never even talked to me about
sex, and they think nobody my age even knows what it is.
My parents think all the guys on my team are so nice and
respectful and innocent, but my parents would die if they
knew what went on in the locker room."

—JAY D. (AGE 14)

"In my younger years, everything I ever learned about sex
I learned in locker rooms. My parents never really talked to
me about it, so the locker room became my sex ed. The
lessons I learned there led me down a dark path of a lot of
broken relationships. I've even got an STD. I only figured out
much later that none of those guys in the locker room knew
what they were talking about. All those older guys on the
team I looked up to as studs and ladies' men are now fat,
drunk, divorced, and hooked on porn. I wish I could unlearn
everything I learned in the locker room."

—DRAKE E. (AGE 31)

In the vacuum created by the lack of healthy conversations
about sex and respect in our homes, churches, and communities, boys are looking for answers online and in locker rooms.
The information they're finding there often creates many
more problems than solutions. Even more dangerous than the
bad information the locker room often provides, it can create a mind-set that there are certain places where it's safe and
acceptable to be disrespectful to women.

As a boy grows into a man, this Locker Room Mentality can give birth to a double life like the tragedy I shared about my friend. When we have any compartment of our lives or our brains where sexist thoughts or actions are allowed to live, it will always cause wreckage. Even if it doesn't lead to an ongoing affair like my friend experienced, it can still rewire a boy's thinking and cause damage to present and future relationships.

The Locker Room Mentality doesn't always take place in an actual locker room. It can happen in a boardroom or a living room or a chat room or simply a hidden room in your own mind where you allow certain thoughts and fantasies to replay on demand. It's really anywhere one or more men create a culture of sexism and disrespect for women under the guise of a healthy, harmless expression of masculinity. The old adage "boys will be boys" has fueled this mentality and given a free pass to generations of men who thought they had the right to be sexist and crude.

I want to clarify that a group of men together doesn't always lead to this mentality. In the previous chapter, I talked about Jesus' example. He was surrounded by a group of male disciples and friends in an environment that was clearly respectful of women. I've seen firsthand the benefits of male groups of friends. I'm not bashing all teams or sports or men's groups. Before you start thinking I'm a buzzkill who is against jokes and having a good time with the guys, I want you to know I believe male friendships can and should be a healthy part of our sons' lives.

I'm not against men getting together and having fun. In

fact, I love it! I'm a guy who loves to tell dumb jokes with the best of them. I was actually voted "Class Clown" of my senior class of college after organizing an *SNL*-style comedy variety show with a group of guys. We were ridiculous and irreverent, but the comedy never crossed the line of being sexist or disrespectful to women. I also love connecting with my two brothers to cut up, enjoy a craft beer, and watch a football game. I've loved being in men's groups, men's Bible studies, sports teams, and even a college fraternity. Ironically, I'm not even against locker rooms. When men are appropriate in their shared celebrations of masculinity and collective team goals, the team environment can be a wonderful place for individual and collective growth. Healthy male friendships are essential.

Even the movies most men like point to our need for male friendships. Ever since my teenage years, my favorite movies have remained *Braveheart* and *Tommy Boy*. One is a movie about epic manly battles, and the other is about ridiculous manly humor. They represent two separate but equal aspects of my own needs, and most men share these same needs for camaraderie, shared battles, and shared laughter. These are healthy needs. We simply need to be more intentional about finding healthy ways to meet these needs instead of settling for dangerous counterfeits.

When done right, there's something so special that happens in a group of male friends. There's nothing like it. There can be a bond of encouragement, accountability, and spurring each other on to great things. The Bible even encourages these relationships with the manly metaphor of swords by saying,

"As iron sharpens iron, so one person sharpens another" (Prov. 27:17 NIV).

I love that verse, and I love the image of godly men being in such close relationship that they're sharpening each other with the clanging sparks of two swords striking each other on the edges, simultaneously sharpening both blades. This is a good and godly pursuit, but somewhere along the way, the modern Locker Room Mentality replaced the heroic, chivalrous, courageous, and pure-hearted brotherhoods of the past.

This is not to say all biblical armies or ancient friendships or heroic knights were perfect. There are plenty of messed-up stories recorded in the Bible and in the history of the age of the knights and Crusades. There are flaws in every man, because all of us have sinned and need the grace of a Savior. The difference between the biblical mandate for manhood and modern complacency with locker room antics isn't that men used to be perfect and now men are bad. It's not the men who have changed, but, rather, our standards for men have changed.

Part of our tacit approval of locker room behavior stems from a lack of acceptable outlets for men to express or celebrate their manhood. Our culture has experienced a collective awakening concerning the mistreatment of women—which is a good thing—but part of our response has been to subtly criticize men and manhood in general—which is a bad thing. This response actually worsens the problem related to the disrespect of women, because it pushes boys and men deeper into the Locker Room Mentality.

I've been surprised by the prevalence of this mentality throughout my own life. I've seen it in every workplace I've been a part of, which includes a pizza restaurant, a grocery store, an automobile factory, a construction site, universities, and even churches. In each of these settings, men who were otherwise "good" men and dedicated husbands and fathers would tell sexist jokes, share sexually explicit stories, and talk about graphic sexual fantasies. I've also heard many sexual and even vulgar comments made by men about their female coworkers.

To cast a ray of light into the darkness and the prevalence of the Locker Room Mentality, please know that not all men participate in this. I've been around many men of great character and integrity who would never participate in or tolerate this kind of behavior. There are many men who display the same levels of honor and integrity both in public and in private. Don't let the bad examples corrupt your view of everyone with a Y chromosome. There are plenty of honorable men out there.

Not all men cave to the pressure to be part of an inappropriate conversation, but for most men it's still a temptation. We never fully outgrow the effects of peer pressure. Even for the men who don't share explicit and sexist words, many of us who are abstainers still lack the courage to speak up and correct the other men by telling them that their words are not okay.

For many years I lacked the courage. For many years I laughed at the jokes or remained silent when a suggestive or outright vulgar comment was made about a woman. It seemed harmless at the time. Why make a big deal? Why create unnecessary awkwardness by calling someone out? My justifications of silent peacemaking were a thin disguise for my cowardice.

Part of my motivation for writing this book is to try to make amends for how my silence has contributed to the crisis I'm now publicly condemning. I want to do better. I want to raise my sons to do better. It's not enough to remain silent when this vile mentality emerges; we must be men of courage who will call men, including ourselves, to a higher standard even if it means being ridiculed or ostracized.

We need to teach our boys that their manhood is a gift to be celebrated, but the collective, chauvinistic celebration of sexual exploits is not a healthy celebration. It's dehumanizing to both the men who participate in it and to the women who are the objects of the sexual jokes, stories, and fantasies. We need an alternative. Author George Gilder has accurately surmised, "Wise societies provide ample means for young men to affirm themselves without afflicting others."[1]

Boys are desperately looking for validation of their manhood. They want to know what it means to be a man. In his book *Searching for Tom Sawyer*, Tim Wright sums up some of the insecurities hiding behind the cocky bravado of locker rooms, boardrooms, and any room where men are settling for a counterfeit version of authentic manhood. He wrote,

> In the United States, proving masculinity appears to be a lifelong project, endless and unrelenting. Daily, grown men call each other out, challenging one another's manhood. And it works most of the time. You can pretty much guarantee starting a fight virtually anywhere in America by questioning someone's manhood.
>
> I've often wondered why must guys test and prove

their masculinity so obsessively? Why do the stakes feel so high? In part, I believe it's because the transitional moment into manhood itself is so poorly defined. We, as a culture, lack any coherent rituals that might demarcate the passage from childhood to adulthood for men or women. Not surprisingly, it also remains unclear who exactly has the authority to do the validating.[2]

Tim Wright's observation goes to the heart of what Robert Lewis addressed in his book *Raising a Modern-Day Knight*: "Communities in the past provided a shared vision of masculinity. They provided ceremonies to mark a boy's passage from adolescence to manhood."[3]

Locker rooms have become a poor substitute for something noble we no longer do. Our boys want to know what it means to be a man, but we've done a convoluted job of defining it for them. We've done an even worse job celebrating it and marking the milestones as they travel from childhood to adolescence and into manhood.

With the lack of any clear definition or rites of passage, boys are left to guess that each birthday is a milestone, or perhaps the appearance of pubic hair or peach fuzz on their chins. These automatic and seemingly superficial marks of manhood do little to satisfy his soul's unspoken question: *Am I a man now?*

This question is the cry of every boy's heart. It starts young. My three-year-old son, Chatham, emerges from the bathroom every time he successfully uses the potty with a confident announcement of his success and then this pronouncement: "I'm becoming a man!"

Even grown men struggle with insecurities over how we measure up. We measure ourselves by murky metrics and always wonder if we're good enough. We wonder if we're good providers, good fathers, and good husbands. We're desperate for respect, and we often feel unworthy of it. In my years of work with married couples, I am convinced the most common unspoken question men constantly ask themselves is, "Does my wife respect me, and does she think I'm a good man?"

If given the choice, most men would rather be respected than loved. Ironically, men are capable of very disrespectful behavior in their quest to be respected. Most men carry wounds of rejection, often from their fathers, and the insecurities left in the aftermath of those wounds can drive a man to even more reckless behavior in an attempt to prove his own manhood and gain respect. Even among arrogant men, there's often a hidden side of insecurity they're attempting to mask through their quest to be the alpha male. We all want to know what a real man really is and how we're measuring up. In the doubt resulting from our ambiguity (or even hostility) surrounding manhood, boys are easy prey for the Locker Room Mentality.

In the locker room, the counterfeit rites of passage emerge as sexual exploits. Instead of tests of character and courage, as was customary in the past, now boys face manhood tests of seduction and prowess. Boys are told their manhood is defined by notches on their belts instead of the timeless truths in their Bibles. Boys are told that girls are prey to be conquered instead of souls to be cherished. When manhood is redefined by the locker room, everyone loses.

So, what are we as parents supposed to do with all this? I'll be addressing the answers to that question in much detail in the upcoming chapters. For this part of the conversation, we first need to acknowledge that the Locker Room Mentality exists, and its temptation is a great pull toward the darker side in the war for our sons' hearts and souls. We need to know that the Locker Room Mentality has temptation only because it promises to meet a need that stems from a healthy desire. Our sons want to know what it means to be a real man, and they're longing for someone to show them what that actually means.

> OUR SONS WANT TO KNOW WHAT IT MEANS TO BE A REAL MAN, AND THEY'RE LONGING FOR SOMEONE TO SHOW THEM WHAT THAT ACTUALLY MEANS.

We need to teach our sons that the Locker Room Mentality is a lie and has no place in healthy manhood. They need to know that it's wrong. They need to know that the more they slip into that misguided mind-set, the more they're sabotaging their current and future relationships with women. They're also doing great harm to themselves. Whenever we use or abuse another human, we sacrifice a part of our own humanity in the process.

IT CAN HAPPEN ANYWHERE

Just this morning, we were watching *Good Morning America* as the kids were getting ready for school. The anchors highlighted yet another story of men abusing and mistreating women. This time, it had happened at a place associated with high class and sophistication, where locker room behavior would seem out of place. As we watched this story unfold, it was a painful reminder that the Locker Room Mentality can happen anywhere.

A nineteen-year-old ballerina named Alexandra Waterbury had dreamed all her life about one day being part of the New York City Ballet, which is considered one of the finest institutions of dance and performing arts anywhere in the world. Her hard work and talent made her dream come true, and she was given a place in the ballet. She soon started dating a twenty-eight-year-old male dancer, and everything in her life seemed perfect. She was in love, or so she thought.

One night at her boyfriend's apartment, she logged on to his laptop to check her email. A thread of text messages from her boyfriend's phone popped up, showing an ongoing correspondence with an unknown number. The text thread referred to her and to other young women in the ballet company with vulgar and derogatory terms. She was shocked and wanted to believe this was some kind of mistake, so she began investigating further.

A few minutes of searching revealed some repugnant discoveries. According to Alexandra, her boyfriend had been photographing her nude without her knowledge and also secretly making video recordings of their lovemaking. He had then been sharing these images and videos with the other male dancers in the ballet company and even with some of the ballet's male donors. At least nine men were part of an underground "Locker Room Network" of men who were using the young women in the ballet company and passing around photos and videos for their collective entertainment.

She was horrified, heartbroken, and enraged all at once. She described how she'd never felt more violated than in that moment. She realized that this man she thought she loved was only using her, and that an entire network of men whom she had trusted was intimately violating her as a sick and twisted form of entertainment.[4]

These men seemed so refined and sophisticated on the surface. By their words and their public actions, they had cunningly crafted reputations as respecters of women, but the insidious Locker Room Mentality had emerged. Behind the scenes, these seemingly sophisticated men were behaving like a secret society of pimps, porn directors, and creepy, clandestine criminals. They were committing a virtual form of rape every time they recorded and shared an intimate image of a woman without the woman's knowledge or consent.

Our thirteen-year-old son was watching this shocking story with us. Part of me wanted to cover his eyes and ears to protect his innocence. I want him to grow up in a world where stories like this don't exist, but I also need to prepare him for a world where this is a daily occurrence. I want him to be equipped with the words and the character traits to know how to respond with wisdom. I want these same things for all my sons and for your kids too. More importantly, God wants these things for our kids.

So, what does it really mean to protect our kids' innocence while not allowing them to live in ignorance of the world's injustices? Jesus taught that we should be "as wise as serpents and as innocent as doves." How do we live out that biblical mandate and teach our children to live in the dichotomy of those two seemingly contradictory extremes?

Jesus wasn't speaking with hyperbole or exaggerated rhetoric when he told us to live with both serpentlike craftiness and dovelike innocence. Balanced parenting requires teaching both lessons within the context of love. I obviously want to protect my boys' innocence, but I also need to temper that innocence with the wisdom that comes from the hard realities of our broken world. It's sometimes a messy and delicate tension between teaching innocence and teaching wisdom, but we must live in that tension to raise children who are equipped for adulthood.

I want my sons to be equipped to address our world's gross injustices and to be part of the solution. This equipping requires countless uncomfortable conversations, but we as parents must have the courage to have those conversations. It's one of the most difficult duties of parenthood, but it's also one of the most rewarding.

Don't let your fear keep you on the sidelines. Ask the hard questions, and have the hard conversations with your sons. If we're not leading the discussion while they're young, we'll have no influence to start the discussion when they're older and more independent. The more you talk, the more they'll listen. The more you listen, the more they'll talk.

Ashley and I used this story as a launchpad into another conversation with Cooper about sexual purity, integrity, and respecting women. We talked candidly to our son about the vile actions that had created this news story we had just watched together. We talked about temptations that other boys and men might place on him someday to justify secret behaviors that are disrespectful (or even criminal) toward women. We talked about integrity, purity, and honesty being hallmarks of authentic manhood. We talked about having the courage to be a protector of women when others are not being respecters of women.

When the story ended and the anchors' conversation turned to weather and sports, we wrapped up our lesson and got up to complete the chaotic morning routine before school started. The entire conversation had only lasted a couple of minutes, and on a morning with four kids getting ready for school, that's about as long as any conversation lasts. After he'd had some time to reflect on the story and on our conversation, he summed up his thoughts in a statement to Ashley. He told his mom, "Those guys should have read Dad's new book. Then they'd understand how important it is to respect women, and this bad story might have never happened."

In the time I've been working on this book, Cooper's off-the-cuff endorsement has been the most significant encouragement to me. Seeing these lessons take root in my own sons' hearts and minds was my primary inspiration for writing in the first place. I hope these lessons continue to take root in them, and despite my countless imperfections and flaws, I hope and pray that my boys see an authentic example of these positive principles in my life. Our kids might forget much of what we say, but they'll never forget whether our words lined up with our actions.

In Women's Own Words

"When men at work treat our meeting rooms like a locker room, I get so uncomfortable. They don't necessarily say anything offensive, but there's this macho vibe they can put off that makes you feel like they're undressing you with their eyes. I don't understand it, but when some men get around other men, they feel like they have to show off by being disrespectful to women. If you really want to 'be the man,' then treat ladies with respect."

—REBECCA C. (AGE 33)

"So many boys in my school want to hook up and expect girls to do sexual stuff for them even if they're not dating each other. If a boy is dating a girl, he totally expects her to do everything (sexually). If a girl doesn't do it, she's labeled as a prude or an ice queen. If she does it, she's labeled as a slut. Either way, I feel like the boys just want our bodies and don't care much about our souls."

—EMILY Z. (AGE 16)

"I wish guys knew that women loved compliments, but we hate creepy compliments. What I mean is that it's nice when a guy recognizes something positive about you, but when all the compliments are about your appearance and he's giving you a head-to-toe look-over when he says it, it's disgusting. It feels like he's undressing me with his eyes. I wish guys would

look me in the eye and compliment me on attributes they would compliment in other men. I don't want to be objectified or rated one-to-ten in their superficial scale. Look me in the eyes and treat me with respect and I'll do the same for you. It's that simple."

—BECCA M. (AGE 20)

"Some men look at women as worthless once we're past the age of being physically desirable in their eyes. Older women should be highly respected, but in some men's eyes, older women are worthless because to them, a woman's value is entirely linked to appearance. Sadly, these superficially minded men miss out on all the wisdom they could learn from ladies with life experience."

—KAREN L. (AGE 61)

"Guys are always putting labels on us. If you play sports, you're a dike. If you study hard, you're a nerd. If you don't laugh at their dirty jokes, you're a snob. Guys believe they can label and define a girl's worth, and so many girls believe the same lie. Only God can define me."

—SARAH R. (AGE 17)

CHAPTER 4

WHAT DOES IT MEAN TO BE A "REAL MAN"?

Be watchful, stand firm in the faith, act like men, be strong.

—1 CORINTHIANS 16:13 ESV

When I was a young boy, I had the privilege of spending some time with my great-grandfather. He was a hardworking farmer who raised nine kids and built a house with his own hands. He never lived to see smartphones, but he probably would have thought grown men playing video games online were wasting their lives!

He was a tough man. His individual knuckles were each

the size of my fist. In his late eighties he still had the strength to take down a young whippersnapper if he wanted to. Despite his rugged strength and grit, he was tenderhearted and kind. He was quick to play with his grandkids, laugh with his friends, kiss his wife, and give a treat to his old mutt, and he'd shed a tear every time he talked about Jesus.

He never made more than five dollars per hour at the union factory in southern Indiana, but before and after each factory shift, he worked hard on his farm so his family would have everything they needed. He hunted or harvested everything his family ate. His closet contained only a few shirts and pairs of overalls, and his earthly possessions were nothing you'd covet, but when he died, he left an estate worth more than a million dollars to his children. Beyond that, though, he left a spiritual legacy of eternal worth that far surpassed that of the money or the land.

We live in a generation now where his brand of manhood might seem antiquated, but we have a lot to learn from his approach. There are many ways that we as modern men are missing the mark. I'm not saying we all have to fit into a narrow definition of masculinity or all be able to handle power tools. After all, my wife is much better with tools than I am. But we need to refocus on some timeless values and guiding principles that will help us become the men we were created to be.

To do that, we first need to open our eyes to some of the most important areas where we as modern men tend to miss the mark. If we will be willing to humbly make course corrections where needed, we could improve our lives, our families, and our legacies.

As an important note, just because you might be currently "failing" in one or more of these areas does not mean you are a failure. *Failure* is not a label you ever need to wear. This book isn't written to assign labels but to call us all to make important corrections in our perceptions and our actions so we can live the most meaningful lives possible.

SEVEN AREAS WHERE MODERN MEN OFTEN MISS THE MARK

Keeping this goal in mind, let's take a look at seven areas where we modern men miss the mark and perhaps unintentionally teach our sons the wrong priorities.

1. We prioritize career and/or hobbies ahead of family.

As men, we tend to be drawn to places that "make sense." In other words, we like our world to have clear rules, roles, and rewards for our actions. In family life, it gets more complicated. We don't always know if we're measuring up. We don't always know what our role should be. It doesn't always make sense. Because of this, many men make the tragic mistake of retreating into their hobbies or careers and trading quality time with family for other pleasures or pursuits. Men: in the end, your family will be all that matters to you. Please don't wait until then to discover this truth. Give them the place of priority they need and deserve in your schedule. They don't need you to be perfect, but they desperately need you to be present!

2. We value our pleasure ahead of our purpose.

We have started valuing porn more than true intimacy, sex more than commitment, and playing the field more than marriage. We're undisciplined in our finances. We're sloppy. We don't want to delay our gratification. We don't want to pursue anything that might cost us something. This daily temptation has the potential to rob us of our very purpose. We have to ask ourselves, *What do I want my life and my legacy to be about? Do I want to only live for the moment, or do I want to make an investment with this moment that will outlive me? Do I want temporary pleasure, or do I want a permanent, positive impact?*

3. We value those who agree with us, but we write off people who don't share our opinions.

We used to live in a society where we could have civil discourse around issues that mattered. Now, whenever someone disagrees with our position, we attack with spiteful vengeance by reducing their argument to an Internet meme and reducing their dignity by name-calling and "un-friending." We are far too quick to label people or put them in boxes. When we refuse to have respectful dialogue around our different convictions and beliefs, we give away a piece of our own humanity, we destroy relationships, and we miss out on the opportunity to learn from anyone who doesn't think and feel exactly like we do. One of the truest tests of mature manhood is the ability to disagree with someone while still remaining respectful.

4. We care more about "getting credit" than having character.

In our success-obsessed culture, we have lost sight of the value of true integrity. Character is measured by what we do when nobody is watching, but these days it seems as if we don't value anything if nobody is watching. We think we can have a closet full of dirty secrets as long as we protect our reputations. We've taken on a shallow and selfish mind-set deserving of the condemnation Jesus gave the Pharisees of his day when he said they were "white-washed tombs that looked good on the outside but were filled with dead men's bones." We need to start valuing integrity over income, character over charisma, and reality over reputation.

5. We elevate our own agenda above everyone else's.

While there's something to be said for having a sense of personal responsibility and work ethic, many of us have taken this too far. We have such a need for control that we push everyone away—including God—if they get in the way of our own agendas. Our need for control creates unnecessary stress or inflated egos, often both. We need to be humble enough to know that there's a God and we're not him. I doubt Drake was rapping about a biblical worldview when he wrote his hit song

WE NEED TO START VALUING INTEGRITY OVER INCOME, CHARACTER OVER CHARISMA, AND REALITY OVER REPUTATION.

"God's Plan," but I hope it reminds listeners that God's plan needs to be the centerpiece of our lives. We need to trust God's plan instead of always forcing our own.

6. *We put ourselves ahead of our wives and set the wrong example for our sons.*

One of the main reasons why boy-girl relationships are so broken is that the examples from so many husband-wife relationships are broken. Many men have redefined what marriage should be using selfish criteria. We often use our wives or make selfish demands instead of truly loving them. Our wives deserve better. Our kids deserve better. If your marriage is struggling and you don't know where to start, please check out the many marriage articles, videos, events, and resources we have available at www.MarriageToday .com.

7. *We value networking over genuine friendships.*

In our quest for personal and professional achievement, we tend to see other people as commodities and assets instead of friends. In the process, we've lost sight of what friendship even means. We find ourselves surrounded by people who owe us favors, but we don't know what it means to do something kind for someone with no thought of repayment. We need to get back to basics. We need to invest in meaningful friendships. Relationships are what give meaning to life. When you and I are on our deathbeds someday, our faith, our families, and our friends will be all that matters.

THE QUEST FOR AUTHENTIC MANHOOD

My wife grew up in a home with one sister and no brothers, and she never watched a sporting event on TV or went to a professional sports game her entire childhood. By contrast, I grew up in a house full of brothers with a dad who had been a football star and even played briefly in the NFL. Sports were in our family's DNA. Even though I was the shortest and least athletic of my brothers, sports still represented a big part of my childhood. When we first started dating, I remember Ashley asking, "Why do guys like sports so much?"

I know that plenty of girls and women love sports every bit as much as men do, so I don't want to make a sexist generalization here, but boys and men are often more inclined toward sports because our testosterone drives us to physical competition. But I don't think that's really the main draw. In response to Ashley's question about men and sports so many years ago, I gave an answer that seemed instinctive. I almost surprised myself with it. It was as if I was lying on a couch in a therapist's office and had discovered a breakthrough moment that helped me make sense of my mental wiring.

I realized I loved sports even though sports really hadn't been good to me. I once threw up while running in the gym in front of the cheerleaders at a baseball tryout. I was cut from the team the next day. I also once threw up at a football practice. My athletic career has produced more vomit than victory! I clearly didn't love sports because of the glory, because I hadn't experienced much of that. I loved sports for a reason I'd never stopped to consider until that moment.

I answered Ashley's question by saying that one of the reasons most guys like sports is because sports make sense. Sports have clear boundaries and clear rules. You can tell by the uniforms who are your allies and who are your adversaries. You can tell by the boundary lines exactly where you're supposed to be. You can tell by the scoreboard whether you're winning. You can tell by the clock exactly how much time you have left to accomplish what needs to be accomplished. You can tell by the umpires or officials who has the authority to intervene when someone breaks a rule. The cheerleaders enthusiastically cheer for you and never criticize you even when you're losing. Your teammates are always your team even when you mess up.

Most men secretly wish all of life had this kind of clarity, and we're constantly tempted to escape the pressures of real life into virtual worlds like fantasy sports leagues where everything seems to make more sense. Even when a man doesn't necessarily like sports, he'll usually be drawn to hobbies or career choices with similar metrics for success. Whether it's playing video games or trading stocks, there are clear rules and clear metrics (or points or dollars) to measure failure and success.

This isn't a justification of men who abandon their responsibilities at home to spend enormous amounts of time on the golf course or playing fantasy football. This isn't an excuse for men who view money or achievements as the primary measures of success, but it's an important nuance of a man's mind that should be understood before we dive in with the exploration of what authentic manhood actually means. Most men want to be a "good man" or a "real man," but we live in a world without clear metrics to determine if we're on the right track or failing.

Despite our hardwired need to find structure and defined success, most men and boys wrestle with insecurities about whether they're succeeding in manhood. Sometimes our obsession with our work or hobbies is nothing more than a distraction to mask the inadequacies we feel with deeper issues. We don't know whether we are succeeding at manhood, because our culture is constantly redefining what manhood really means. We've lost sight of what it means to be a real man, or if such a thing even exists.

I chuckle at the irony of me writing a chapter on what it means to be a real man, because a recently diagnosed thyroid disorder has caused my testosterone levels to plummet. Even with my normal testosterone levels, I've never been able to grow a full beard, and I look like a middle school kid with patches and peach fuzz when I try! I can count my chest hairs on one hand, but I'm getting to the age where I'm now growing hair in all kinds of places where I don't want it. That's probably more information than you wanted about my body hair.

So, if testosterone levels aren't the most accurate indicator of real manhood, then what is? I believe most of us are defining manhood (and womanhood) by superficial, unrealistic terms. As you've probably noticed, our world is pretty quick to judge people by their outward appearance. I was at my six-year-old son's first baseball practice today, and one of the other kids was commenting on batters taking turns hitting the ball.

He said wisely, "You can't tell who's going to be good by how they look."

Some kids who looked the part and had all the right base-ball gear would get up to the plate and strike out with clumsy swings. Other kids who were short or unintimidating in their physical presence might get up to the plate and reveal a sharp skill honed with many hours of practice in the backyard with their dads.

I wish we as adults had the wisdom of this six-year-old kid to know that you can't tell if someone is good just by how they look. In a world that celebrates superficialities and attempts to define people in shallow terms, I try to remind myself that God's opinion is the only one that really counts, and 1 Samuel 16:7 tells us, "People judge by outer appearance, but the LORD looks at the heart."

Authentic manhood is, of course, about much more than testosterone levels or height or appearance or athletic ability. People may prejudge you based on your appearance, and blood tests can measure your hormones, but there's no blood test that can measure a man's integrity and character. I want my sons to know that being a real man is about so much more than macho bravado; it's about honor and respect. Real men respect women, and real men respect themselves too.

There are certainly great men all around us, but there also seems to be a growing void created by men who are abandon-ing their responsibilities and leaving women and children to fend for themselves. In Japan, there's a new product that creates a moving shadow of a man on the walls of a house to protect women who are home alone by giving would-be intruders the warning that a man is home watching over the place.[1] It may be a practical product, but in some ways I also see it as a sad commentary on life. Authentic manhood is being replaced by a mere shadow of the real thing, and the absence of men forces women and children to have to settle for shadows.

Too many men are absent either physically or emotionally. Respect begins with presence. Men must stop running from responsibility and start running toward it. Men must stop running from difficulties and start taking responsibility to resolve the difficulties.

Of course, some men stay present for the wrong reasons, and their absence might be welcomed. When a man misunderstands what manhood really means, there's so much pain that can be inflicted on those in his orbit. When I look at the pervasive disrespect for women and sexual objectification of women in our culture, I'm convinced one of the root causes is that we've lost sight of what honorable manhood really means. We've believed the myth that we can define gender as anything we want it to be, so a natural digression of that flawed logic means we also get to define manhood on our own terms.

In the void of any cultural absolutes or moral authority, many boys and men have created an unwritten value system based on the most primal aspects of masculinity. Instead of valuing sexual restraint and monogamy, we celebrate the sexual prowess and promiscuity of men who can indiscriminately seduce countless women.

Instead of valuing humility, we celebrate arrogance. Just listen to the lyrics of the most popular songs. The men we idolize as music moguls are often singing about the objectification

of women, a disregard for the law or any authority, and a celebration of vain materialism.

Instead of service, we celebrate being served. Even those
of us who follow Christ tend to whitewash his bold teachings
about serving others, and instead, we measure our greatness
by how many people are serving us. We've forgotten that anyone who is unwilling to hold a door or a mop is unfit to hold
a microphone or a position of leadership.

Instead of valuing responsibility or maturity, we celebrate
the rebels who boast in their lack of accountability to anyone.
We ignore the voices of wisdom and hand microphones to
foolish scoffers who mock and curse and rage against everything and yet never take action or make personal sacrifices to
make things better.

Our culture is caught in a civil war where one half seems
to be doing battle against men and the other half seems to
be feverishly working to redefine manhood. Neither of these
approaches will bring lasting results. Male bashing won't pro-
duce better results, and neither will a futile attempt to redefine
manhood in light of our ever-changing agendas and ideas
about political correctness.

We don't need a new definition of manhood. We need to
return to a timeless, biblical definition of manhood and then
find ways to help our boys live out that brand of authentic
manhood in our modern culture. When I watch the news or
Netflix, I can easily get confused by what manhood is supposed
to be, but when I read the Bible it all becomes crystal clear.

With that clarity as our goal, let's spend the remainder of
this chapter clearly identifying some cornerstones of manhood

outlined in the Bible and then discuss how we can help our sons aspire to these traits in their own lives.

7 LESSONS THAT TURN A BOY INTO A MAN

I want my boys to have an understanding of people's emotions, their insecurities, people's distress, and their hopes and dreams.

—PRINCESS DIANA

Since God has entrusted me with the sacred duty of raising four boys to noble manhood, I want to make sure I'm teaching them the right lessons! They're growing up in a world where manhood has been redefined and good role models are harder to come by. I want my boys to know that they're not automatically a man just because they start shaving or hit their eighteenth birthday. Manhood is about so much more than hair and age. Ashley and I want to help our boys mark the journey to manhood with some milestone moments we can share together.

In our family we've created rites of passage as our boys enter adolescence. Inspired by author Bob Goff's family policy of taking kids on adventurous pilgrimages when they are ten years old, we've instituted something similar. The year that each of our boys turns ten, they get to pick any spot in the USA and go on a trip with their mom. The year they turn twelve, they go on a missions trip to Casa Shalom Orphanage in Guatemala.

The year our boys turn thirteen we plan something very

special. Thirteen is the age some cultures recognize adulthood, including Jewish culture, where boys have an elaborate Bar Mitzvah celebration. In our family, the year the boys turn thirteen, they get to go on an international trip with me to any place they choose. My oldest son, Cooper, chose London, England, and we are heading there later this week. We've both been looking forward to this trip for years!

As the boys get older, we'll plan other rites of passage to celebrate milestones. These events don't need to look the same in every family, but I'd highly recommend making an intentional plan in your own family. Celebrate those moments, and make sure you are creating profound milestones and memories with your kids. It might take some budgeting and some planning, but I promise it's well worth it. Our family's favorite pictures on display and the favorite stories we tell come from our shared adventures. These adventures are also an opportunity for us to reteach lessons about faith, family, respect, and what it really means to be a man.

As I've mentioned already, modern ideals of masculinity are a mixture of unrealistic or even destructive role models. Hip-hop culture often presents a man as lawless, materialistic, and womanizing, with no respect for authority. This is particularly damaging for audiences in settings where fathers are largely absent. Those boys are looking for role models, and, sadly, when there's not one at home, the ones on the radio and on TV often fill the void.

Mainstream media paints the picture of ideal manhood in drastically different ways. One minute a man is being told to reject his masculinity and take on a vision of modern family dynamics where there is virtually no distinction between men and women apart from genitalia. The next minute, men are being told to "man up," which can mean anything from eating more red meat and lifting weights to working longer hours to provide the American dream for the family.

With so many conflicting messages and so few healthy outlets for expressing genuine manhood, many guys escape into their "man cave" or into the cyber world of video games, porn, stock trading, or fantasy football. I don't want that for my boys. I want them to be the courageous men God created them to be—and not only in a fantasy world. I don't want to raise them with an idea of manhood that's based on my own opinions or the ever-changing opinions of culture. I want them to learn the truths of manhood from the One who created men in the first place.

So how does Scripture define genuine manhood? To help us gain clarity and establish a shared foundation, I'll share the definition I've derived from my study on this topic. It's a definition I aspire to daily and one I'm trying to model for my sons as I teach them to do the same.

> A genuine man is one who courageously fights for what's right, selflessly seeks responsibility, works hard to provide for himself and others, practices self-discipline, respects women and respects other men, lives with integrity, and trusts God as his loving Father and his final authority in all things.

Every aspect of this definition is important, but it will make more sense if we dissect it and examine one principle at a time. Let's divide this definition into seven timeless truths from God's Word about the duties of a man, which have universal application to all men in all cultures. These are the tenets I hope to teach and model for my sons.

1. *Have the courage to fight for what's right.*

Being a man doesn't mean you have to go around punching people as if you're in an Ultimate Fighting Championship cage match, but it does mean you must have the courage to take a stand for what's right. Speak up for the powerless. Defend the weak. Fight for justice for the oppressed. Fight for your family.

> Don't be afraid of them. Remember the Lord, who is great and awesome, and fight for your families, your sons and your daughters, your wives and your homes. (Neh. 4:14 NIV)

2. *Seek responsibility instead of running from it.*

Boys run from responsibility; men run toward responsibility. If you're a grown man living in your parents' basement and constantly bouncing around between different women and dead-end jobs, you're not a man. You're a boy with a beard. Grow up.

> A wise son brings joy to his father, but a foolish son brings grief to his mother. (Prov. 10:1 NIV)

3. *Work hard at whatever you do, and when you have a family, work hard to provide for them.*

Your wife and your children should know that you would be willing to go hungry to make sure they're fed. It's not the government's job to feed your family. It's *your* job. There's no shame in assistance when you need it, but you should also be willing to work hard to provide.

Those unwilling to work will not get to eat. (2 Thess. 3:10)

4. Show patience and restraint. Don't be ruled by your temper or your temptations.

Remember that one of the biggest biblical distinctions between a wise person and a fool is the ability to show restraint and not be controlled by your temper or your need for instant gratification. Emotions are a tool given by God, and there are healthy and important ways to express them, but don't be ruled by them. If you don't learn to master your anger and your emotions, then your anger and emotions will master you.

Fools vent their anger, but the wise quietly hold it back. (Prov. 29:11)

5. Respect your wife before you meet her by keeping yourself from sexual sin. Respect your wife after you're married by remaining faithful, respectful, and loving in all circumstances.

In many ways, your life and legacy will be defined by how you love your wife. Respect all women, but respect your wife most of all. She deserves your best and not what's left over after you've given your best to everyone and everything else. Show her you'd be willing to lay down your life for her. When you become a husband and a father, show your boys what it means to love and respect a wife, because they're learning what marriage means by watching you.

> Husbands, love your wives, just as Christ loved the church and gave himself up for her. (Eph. 5:25 NIV)

6. Keep your word and honor your commitments.

Fulfill your commitments. This is the essence of manhood. Pay your debts, keep your word, and always speak the truth. When you've blown it, admit it and seek forgiveness. Be a man of integrity, which simply means being honest, dependable, and the same person in public and in private. Don't make your decisions based on your feelings; make your choices based on your commitments.

> Who keeps an oath even when it hurts. (Ps. 15:4 NIV)

7. Trust God. Let his Word be the road map of your life.

God made you, and his plan for your life is the only plan that counts. Don't be so prideful that you try to do it on your own. Life is meant to be lived in relationship with your Creator. If you're walking with him, you'll always be headed in the right direction! If your feelings ever conflict with what's written in the Bible, then your feelings are wrong. The Bible will never steer you in the wrong direction. The more you learn God's Word and trust God's Word, the more the Holy Spirit will shape your character, making you more and more like Jesus.

Trust in the LORD with all your heart; do not depend on your own understanding. Seek his will in all you do, and he will show you which path to take. (Prov. 3:5–6)

All seven of the scriptures listed above would be good to memorize with your son. Planting God's Word in your mind and heart provides a compass for your character. The Bible also says, "I have hidden your word in my heart, that I might not sin against you" (Ps. 119:11).

WHEN YOU FEEL LIKE YOU'RE FAILING AS A PARENT, REMEMBER THIS . . .

Maybe you're reading all of this and, instead of finding encouragement in these words, you're feeling guilty. You're feeling like you've blown it and somehow already ruined your kids beyond all repair. You see an indictment of your own shortcomings in the previous list about ways men are falling short. Maybe you're a mom reading this, and you're feeling guilty because of mistakes you've made or mistakes you've allowed to be made by your husband (or by the lack of a father figure in your son's life). Perhaps you are tempted to throw this book aside, pour yourself a tall glass of wine, and resign yourself to the fact that you're never going to be a good parent.

We've all felt like that at times. Please don't let the discouragement keep you from moving forward. Being a parent is probably the most difficult but also the most rewarding job on the planet. It's a sacred duty, a 24-7 job, a potentially terrifying responsibility, and a legacy-defining work. With all the pressures that come with such a big job, we parents tend to beat ourselves up too easily over our blunders. Here's a little perspective that's helped me on those days when I feel like I'm failing as a parent, which happens almost daily.

When you feel like you're failing, consider that Jesus' earthly parents lost him for three days while they were on a road trip. The entire first day they didn't even know he was lost! Seriously. You can look up the story in the Bible. We name statues and cathedrals after Joseph and Mary, but you feel guilty when you lose your kid at Walmart for ten minutes! Give yourself some grace.

As parents, we tend to take way too much credit when our kids do something right and way too much blame when our kids do something wrong. I've known plenty of people who thought they were amazing parents because their first kid was naturally a "pleaser" with a more docile, compliant personality. They judged other parents with rambunctious kids until they had a strong-willed kid of their own! Our kids' behavior—positive or negative—isn't always the result of our parenting. If you don't believe me, consider the fact that God is a perfect Father, and yet his kids (that's us) make bad choices every day.

Each child is masterfully unique. It's our sacred responsibility to love, equip, encourage, discipline, and guide each one toward responsible adulthood. It's not our job to raise good kids; it's our job to raise responsible adults and to invest in our relationship with them so they still want to see us when they grow up and don't have to see us anymore. This doesn't mean being a child's buddy or "BFF" is more important than being his or her parent. It just means that, to quote Dr. James Dobson, "Rules without relationships lead to rebellion."

Keep learning and growing and striving as a parent, because the most important work you will ever do will be within the walls of your own home. Celebrate the beautiful moments along the way, and on those days when you feel like you've failed as a parent, give yourself some grace. Your parents were far from perfect, and you still turned out awesome!

So, armed with some fresh encouragement and perspective, how do we chart a course for our sons? How do we help them overcome their past shortcomings and our own shortcomings too? The coming chapters will focus on ways to help our sons become the men of honor and integrity God created them to be. As a parent, you have much more influence in his life than you might realize. You are helping to shape the man he will become someday.

> THE MOST IMPORTANT WORK YOU WILL EVER DO WILL BE WITHIN THE WALLS OF YOUR OWN HOME.

In Women's Own Words

"The strongest man I ever knew was my dad. He was injured in Vietnam and was permanently disabled. He showed me that a man's real strength doesn't come from the size of his muscles but from the size of his commitment to his faith and his family. I want my own sons to have the character and courage of their Granddaddy when they grow up."

—MYRA O. (AGE 44)

"A real man respects women. A bad man uses women. It's really that simple."

—KIM Y. (AGE 51)

"The boys in my middle school can be so gross, but they can also be nice. I like being friends with boys because they're less drama than girl groups, but then sometimes my guy friends will say stuff that just makes me really uncomfortable."

—ABBY A. (AGE 13)

"We are five!! One woman versus four men (not fair, ha ha). I feel disrespected when nobody waits for me. They start walking and I'm the last one. Also when we go to the movies and they just want to watch superhero movies and nobody cares which one I want to watch. I feel respected when they open the door and wait for me. When they watch a movie I like and feel they care."

—PERLA R. (AGE 39)

CHAPTER 5

THE NAKED TRUTH ABOUT SEX

Run from sexual sin! No other sin so clearly affects the body as this one does. For sexual immorality is a sin against your own body.

—1 CORINTHIANS 6:18 NLT

A couple of years ago, my oldest son, Cooper, was entering into adolescence, and it was time to have a serious talk about sex. Ashley and I have always been open with the boys, trying to take the shock and scandal out of sex conversations. In age-appropriate ways, we try to keep an open dialogue around changing bodies, changing hormones, mixed messages about sex in culture, and God's plan for sex in Scripture. We want to be the first place our kids turn to when they have questions about sex, instead of starting with Google or friends on the school bus.

All these little conversations along the way finally culminated in the granddaddy of all sex talks. I wasn't sure if I was ready or if he was ready, but I'd put it off long enough. I called in some backup in the form of ordering the "Passport2Purity" CDs from FamilyLife Today.[1] As a quick, unsolicited endorsement, I'll tell you these CDs were an excellent resource, and I'd highly recommend them to any parent who wants to have a healthy dialogue about sex with their kids.

Cooper and I started our overnight manly road trip, and, with sweaty palms and a racing heartbeat, I put in the first CD. I had already given him fair warning that we'd be talking a lot about sex over the next couple of days, and he was dreading it even more than I was. I tried to stay upbeat, but I think he could tell I was nervous. I felt like an awkward middle school kid all over again as that first CD started playing.

I tried to keep my eyes straight on the road for as long as I could, and Cooper did the same. I think it was as long as either of us had ever gone without making eye contact with someone. We finally reached the first break in the CD, when we were supposed to spend time talking about what we'd just heard. I worked up some forced enthusiasm and said, "Hey, buddy! What did you think about that? A lot of good info, huh?"

As I turned to see his response, he had his head buried by his knees with his hands over his head. He had the posture of someone who was puking on an airplane. I waited a moment to make sure he wasn't actually puking. Then I waited another moment to make sure I wasn't going to puke. Neither of us puked.

We both regained our composure, laughed off the awkwardness, and launched into meaningful conversations about God's perfect plan for the gift of sex and how that plan has been hijacked, misused, and redefined by a culture searching for meaning and pleasure apart from God. We talked about the joy of sex when it's expressed within a healthy marriage and the negative aftermath of sex when it's used casually.

We talked about how sex should always be rooted in respect. When we choose to misuse sex, we're disrespecting ourselves, we're disrespecting our sexual partners, and we are disrespecting the God who created sex and created us in his own image. Everyone gets hurt as a result. When respect for God's laws, respect for our own bodies, and respect for God's daughters is at the forefront of our thinking, we'll no longer be asking, "How far can I go without getting into trouble?" Instead, we'll be asking, "How can I show more respect to my Creator and to the women he made in his own image?" If we'll take that approach, we'll be able to enjoy the standard for sexuality the apostle Paul gave to all Christians when he said, "Among you there must not be even a hint of sexual immorality" (Eph. 5:3 NIV).

I want my sons to adopt the sexual standards of the Bible, which are concisely summarized in the book *Every Young Man's Battle* with this profound promise of purity: "Sexual purity is receiving no sexual gratification from anything or anyone outside of your spouse."[2]

That's a high standard, but it's the right standard. If we teach our sons to follow it, they'll prevent so much unnecessary pain in their own lives and in the lives of the young ladies they date before marriage. I want this desire for sexual purity to grip my sons' hearts and become so much more than a rule to follow. I want them to see sexual purity as a lifestyle of honor.

I don't want my boys to try to maintain sexual purity out of some misguided form of legalism where they're attempting to earn God's favor. Legalism is focused on breaking God's rules, but true faith is much more concerned with breaking God's heart and breaking the hearts of those who would be harmed by our sin. God's redemptive plan is always rooted in healthy relationships, and if we're misusing sex, we're unleashing a great destroyer of healthy relationships. We should make every decision, including decisions about sex, in light of what will promote relational health and healing with God and with others.

When you look around our current culture, everywhere you turn there are examples of people misusing God's gift of sex. The notion that sex is created for a lifelong, monogamous commitment between one husband and one wife is treated with contempt as an archaic and out-of-touch approach. Under the guise of enlightenment and progress, we've defined sex on our own terms and then ignored the obvious consequences our sexual rebellion has created.

I want to share an example from history about a group of people with good ideas and good motives who completely missed the point when it came to sex. In missing the point about sex, their movement died altogether. Instead of erring on the modern extreme of promiscuity, they made the mistake of championing chastity to the point of believing all sex was wrong.

WHEN "SEX" BECOMES A DIRTY WORD

"I wish my parents would talk to me about sex. I mean, I'm sure it would gross me out at first just to hear either of them say the word, but I hear so many different things at school about it, and I look at porn mostly just as an educational tool so that if I ever get with a girl I'll actually know what I'm supposed to do. Whenever sex is mentioned at my house on TV or anything, my parents just say something about how that's 'dirty' and we shouldn't talk about things like that. I guess that means I'm supposed to figure it out on my own."

—BILLY A. (AGE 15)

In the heart of the idyllic Bluegrass region of central Kentucky, nestled in the midst of rolling fields and picturesque horse farms, you'll find a quaint settlement of houses that looks like a movie set capturing small-town life in the 1800s. I find myself humming the theme song to *Little House on the Prairie* every time I'm there. This pristinely preserved collection of centuries-old buildings is called Shaker Village of Pleasant Hill. It's known to the locals simply as Shakertown.

Growing up in Central Kentucky, I was surrounded by natural beauty and horse farms, but there weren't an abundance of exciting tourist destinations, so Shakertown stood out as something novel. Nearly every year of my childhood, our public schools made a field trip to see it and learn the history of this unique and mysterious group known as the Shakers.

The Shakers were pioneers in gender equality and creating an egalitarian community where men and women shared the responsibilities of leadership with no stigmas or limitations defining what a girl could grow up to become. Centuries ago, their ideas were radical and revolutionary.

There's much to applaud about the Shakers. Their work ethic and craftsmanship were unparalleled. They saw their work as a form of worship and did everything to the glory of God. This commitment to excellence is probably why their buildings and even much of their furniture endures centuries after being built.

We can also commend their desire to live out their Christian faith as a community of equality. They chose to see inherent value in every person and recognized all people, men and women, as being of equal worth and coheirs as sons and daughters in God's kingdom. In that way, their lifestyle was a tiny glimpse of heaven.

For all the many positive attributes we can see in the Shakers, there were also some very troubling aspects of their belief system. While they championed the value and equality of women in a time when so few shared those sentiments, they didn't value marriage. Without a healthy view of marriage, they sabotaged their otherwise healthy views of respect for women.

When a married couple decided to join the Shakers, they

had to enter the community as a brother and sister in Christ and as a brother and sister with the others in the village. They were no longer allowed to function as a married couple. The Shakers required strict separation of men and women. While both men and women shared in leadership and were treated with equality, they were also treated separately.

Men and women lived in separate buildings. They ate at separate tables. They worshiped on separate sides of the sanctuary. They even had separate doors for entering and exiting. They also didn't believe in sex. My dad always joked that's why they were always shaking: sexual frustration!

The Shakers sought equality through separation. In this they missed the mark, because true equality can only exist within the context of healthy relationships. We can never find true equality apart from relationships because they are the whole purpose of life.

You can admire someone without knowing them or interacting with them. I admire plenty of famous people I'll never meet, but respect and love are different. Respect and love can't exist apart from relationships. They're not abstract concepts, but real-life expressions of our souls that can only be given and received from real-life people in real-life ways.

I want my sons to grow up with a sincere love and respect for the girls and women in their lives. This type of love and respect doesn't just happen through healthy beliefs; it always requires healthy relationships.

> WE CAN NEVER FIND TRUE EQUALITY APART FROM RELATIONSHIPS.

It's probably no surprise to you that the Shakers movement died out, and all that remains are the remnants of their
buildings and handmade furniture and schoolchildren on
field trips learning about their strange way of life. It turns out
that forcing celibacy isn't a great recruitment tool, and it also
does nothing to create future generations through childbear-
ing. Still, it's a beautiful place to visit if you ever find yourself
in Central Kentucky.

I want to be part of a movement that shares the Shakers'
vision for gender equality but finds ways to live out that vision
in relationships instead of in segregation. As it relates to raising my sons, I want them to see that true respect for women
must exist in healthy relationships with women. In school,
in the workplace, in friendships, and eventually in marriage,
respect for women doesn't happen from a distance; it happens
in relationships.

I also want them to know that when we avoid talking about
sex, nobody wins. In the vacuum our silence creates, people are
either tempted to demonize sex and miss out on the God-given
beauty of it in marriage, or they may go to the other extreme and
live a life of promiscuity. Sex is a powerful gift, and when misused, it can create great pain and disrespect. But when enjoyed
in the right context, it's one of the greatest gifts God has given us.

SEX ON CAMPUS

Sex and respect are inextricably tied together. A misguided view
of sex or a hedonistic pursuit of sex can cause immeasurable

pain, regret, and relational baggage. When we don't train our sons and daughters to see the sacredness of sexuality through the lens of God's standards, they may be more at risk of sabotaging their future relationships. When parents are silent on these issues, kids go off to college vulnerable to temptation and reckless forms of sexual experimentation. These sexual escapades can't be casually brushed aside as a "sowing wild oats" rite of passage. No, these disrespectful sexual missteps can create some of the most painful scars imaginable.

Just down the road from Shakertown in a Communication Studies graduate course on the University of Kentucky campus, I remember sitting around a circle with other graduate students, listening with shock to the new research findings of our professor. Dr. Alan D. DeSantis was one of the most talented, entertaining, and eclectic educators I ever had. He was also an advisor for some of the fraternities and sororities on campus, and he was leveraging his knowledge of Greek life—as a former frat guy himself and now as an advisor—to do an in-depth analysis of gender roles and sexual behaviors of modern college students in fraternities and sororities. His research opened my eyes to the widespread culture of sex-based disrespect happening on university campuses.

He started the discussion by explaining that there had been a long history in fraternities of organizing events, often under the guise of social mixers or fundraisers, with the primary objective of convincing young women to perform for them. In other words, the frat boys felt entitled to disrespect these young women all in the name of fun and entertainment. This performance-based expectation of females also often crossed lines into expectations of sexual performance. He later summed up all these findings in a groundbreaking research study and book entitled *Inside Greek U.: Fraternities, Sororities, and the Pursuit of Pleasure, Power, and Prestige.*[3]

Of all the findings his multiyear research yielded, none was more troubling than the sexual climate on campus and specifically the sexual objectification of women. College men seemed pleased to play the role of a feminist, and then, under the guise of female empowerment, these men would pour strong drinks, create festive atmospheres, and do whatever they could to bed as many young women as possible.

Even when intercourse wasn't taking place, young men became crafty in the art of coercion by convincing young women to perform other sexual acts, such as oral sex and anal sex. These men would use a woman's body for their own sexual gratification while at the same time praising the young woman for her chastity, class, and "technical virginity."

These findings about the sexual status quo on college campuses are even more troubling when combined with the stats we went over earlier about how one in five women are the victims of sexual assault and how 30 percent of college-aged men confessed they'd be willing to commit rape if they knew they could get away with it. Dr. DeSantis's research results were also in line with comments I heard while studying and teaching at multiple universities. Those times unearthed troubling statements like these:

> "The more classy a girl is in public, the more she wants to be treated like a whore in the bedroom. It's all a game. I

treat classy girls like whores and I treat whores like classy girls. It takes their guards down, and they end up doing whatever I want in the bedroom."

—CHASE E. (AGE 21)

"Most girls don't actually mean 'no' when they say it. The hard-to-get routine is all part of the seduction. They act un-willing just because they know it's a turn-on for a guy if the girl seems like more of a challenge. They also want to have it both ways: they want sex as much as guys do, but they also want to be seen as proper or whatever. Girls want sex even if they say they don't."

—JAKE K. (AGE 20)

Statements like the above should be horrifying to parents of girls and parents of boys as well. Even with all the political and policy attention being directed at these issues on university campuses, the problems persist, because it takes more than policy changes to make a difference. It takes a heart change.

I was on a college campus recently, and I saw a young woman wearing a shirt with the slogan "Got Consent?" It has become a popular campaign on campuses to try to turn the tide of sexual assault and unwanted sexual aggression toward women. On the same day, a guy with a sick and inappropriate sense of humor wore another popular fraternity T-shirt slo-gan, which seems to be an inappropriate, misogynistic, and misguided counterpoint to the "Got Consent?" campaign. His shirt said, "No means Yes. Yes means Anal!"

For all you parents of younger kids reading this, I promise

I'm not trying to terrify you with these extreme examples of sexual brokenness on our university campuses. I'm not trying to convince you to homeschool your kids until they're thirty years old. I understand the instinct we have to protect our children, but we also need to prepare our children to live out their faith and values in a broken world.

The good news is that there are many young men and women in both Christian universities and secular ones who are living with respect for each other, with sexual purity and with integrity. There are many whose testimonies will never include the dark chapters that result from sexual compromise. There are plenty of good kids out there, and even among those who have made compromises or fallen into a cycle of sexual sin, God's grace is always bigger than our biggest sin. Those poor choices don't have to define anyone's future.

Here's the best news of all: Your kids can be among those who grow up to make wise choices related to sex. Your kids can leave the relative safety of your home and venture out into the world as young adults equipped to handle the temptations and traps that can so easily ensnare the unprepared. Your kids can do it right, but it starts with you and having the courage to have healthy conversations about sex.

It's not our job to terrify our kids about sex. It's not our job to keep our kids cloistered in an artificial reality where sex doesn't exist. It's not our job to move to Shakertown and convert to a religion where sex is never talked about or presented as an option. It's not our job to quit the conversation the moment our kids have the basic biological knowledge of the procreating functions of a penis and a vagina.

We must have the courage to lead healthy conversations about sex. Our conversations can't just be fixated on genitals and STDs. There's no condom that can protect the soul. We must talk about the oneness and spiritual connection God intended when he created the beautiful gift of sex. We must talk about the rapturous joys of sex when enjoyed in a monogamous marriage, but we must also give sober warnings about the pitfalls of sex when used in inappropriate contexts. We must be willing to wade into the minefield of teaching lessons from our own sexual pasts and possible poor choices. If we won't do it, in the vacuum created by our silence, our kids will always get the wrong messages.

NAKED AND UNASHAMED

Far too many parents and churches and educators have taught an untrue and harmful message about sex. In an attempt to keep kids from delving into risky, early sexual exploration, sex itself is often demonized in our discussions. Throughout this book (particularly in the chapters on masturbation and porn), I'll share in fairly explicit detail the pitfalls of misusing sex, but avoiding the bad is only half the discussion—and I'd argue it is the less-important half. Once people get a glimpse of God's perfect plan for sex, the quest for his best gifts will make the counterfeits of sexual sin seem unattractive in comparison.

A promiscuous lifestyle certainly should be avoided at all costs, but in our pious attempt to avoid promiscuity, we've thrown the proverbial baby out with the bathwater and have adopted a Shaker-like condemnation of all sex. As parents, we must teach our kids about sex in a healthy way and start the conversations focusing on the positive. We need to stop making *sex* a dirty word.

Sometimes we do this subconsciously. When we see a steamy image flash across the TV screen, instead of taking the time to explain why that's an inappropriate display of sexuality and how sexualizing others should not be a form of our own entertainment, we just label it as "disgusting" or "trashy" and then turn the channel. Without understanding the broader context that God's plan for sex is beautiful, kids can grow up seeing sex as something negative, and then when they start having sexual feelings, they'll believe there's something wrong with them.

> WE MUST TEACH OUR KIDS ABOUT SEX IN A HEALTHY WAY AND START THE CONVERSATIONS FOCUSING ON THE POSITIVE.

This sets up our kids for sexual failure and shame. I know it's easier to slap a negative label on something than it is to have a dialogue that might lead to awkward questions and possibly even confessions about our own sexual history and past sins. That's scary, but it's worth the awkwardness to help our kids discover what it means to be "naked and unashamed."

I didn't come up with this phrase, "naked and unashamed." It's actually God's idea. All great ideas are really his. We might try to reword things or get retweeted for saying something clever, but he's the Creator of all good things, including sex.

When God first created man and woman in his own image, he made the man and his wife naked, and the Bible tells us in Genesis 2:24 that they were naked and unashamed. I love that imagery. I love that one of the first lessons the Bible teaches is that God has a beautiful plan for sex and marriage, and while deceivers might do much damage in creating counterfeit plans for sex, God's timeless design is still for complete love, intimacy, vulnerability, pleasure, acceptance, and joy. He still wants us to be naked and unashamed.

Ashley and I talk about this concept often in our marriage ministry. At marriage conferences and churches all over America, we've talked to couples about our own story, our hang-ups and baggage, and God's redemptive love and grace in our marriage. We get vulnerable with others to help husbands and wives find the courage to get vulnerable with each other. (Don't worry. We don't actually get naked in front of anybody but each other!)

We believe that a "naked" marriage isn't just physical. The Bible's imagery of nakedness applies to all aspects of life. Nakedness is a picture of transparency and vulnerability. God wants us to enter marriage with no secrets and nothing to hide. He wants us with nothing up our sleeves, because we're not wearing any sleeves! That's what I want for my sons and for the women they'll grow up to marry someday. That's what I want for your sons and daughters, too, because it's what God wants for all his kids.

RAISING BOYS WHO RESPECT GIRLS

NAKED AND SHAMELESS

Some of us struggle to ever discover the joys of being naked and unashamed, because we've allowed the pendulum to swing far in the other direction and become naked and shameless. What I mean is that our world has a way of desensitizing us to God's truth and searing our consciences until we no longer feel holy conviction when we're doing destructive behaviors.

If you touch a hot stove long enough, you will burn off your nerve endings and won't feel the pain anymore, even though great damage is still being done. It can work this way on an emotional and spiritual level, not just a physical one. Our conscience's "nerve endings" can stop working when we get into a perpetual habit of ignoring God's voice.

When this happens with sexual sin, instead of becoming naked and unashamed, we can become naked and shameless. We might not be feeling shame, but it's not out of innocence and intimacy. It's out of callousness. The subtle voice of pride starts whispering lies to us like, "You can do whatever you want. You don't have to answer to anybody. Do what feels right. How can it be wrong if it feels so good? Nobody is going to get hurt."

When we start believing the lies, we're in trouble. I want my sons to know that pride is a sin. It's not only a sin in and of itself but pride is the soil where all other sin takes root.

Part of the problem of pride might be on your end as a parent. Pride can creep in when we are not willing to have honest conversations about sex, because we're afraid to divulge too much of our own past sexual choices. We don't want our kids to feel justified to have sex because of our poor example, or maybe we just want to maintain an aura of moral superiority by allowing our kids to live in the illusion that we've never sinned.

I recently read an article by Roland Warren where he shared some of his own experience with this complicated issue of knowing how much to share with our kids. Roland explained that he had become a father while still a teenager, and his own father had done the same thing. Roland was embarrassed by his actions, and he wanted his own children to break the family cycle of teenage parenthood, but he knew he'd need courage to confess his shortcomings to his children as part of the lesson he was teaching them. Roland explained his reasoning here:

> If you try to admonish your children to stop doing something that is immoral or illegal while you continue to do so, you are being a hypocrite. And, most likely your kids will call you on it. However, spiritual growth is when you tell your children to not do something that you once did and you learned was not God's best for you or that violated God's principles. This is like a parent saying, "once I was blind but now I see." Indeed, a blind man who receives his sight and helps others avoid a dangerous ditch that he once stumbled into is not a hypocrite. He's a hero. So, too, are parents who protect their children from repeating mistakes they made in the past.[4]

Roland's perspective challenged me to be completely honest with my own sons about both the wise choices and the foolish choices. When we follow God's perfect plans for sex, there are blessings for everyone. When we follow our own lustful inclinations or when we compromise by following the culture's ever-changing sexual standards, everyone gets hurt. When we stay silent about these things and expect our kids to figure it out on their own, they'll get hurt. These difficult conversations might prove to be some of the most meaningful words you'll ever exchange with your kids. Have the courage to do it.

I want my sons to know they can be naked and unashamed with their wives someday, but I also want them to know that nakedness with women outside the context of marriage should bring a very different response. This obviously relates to the dangers of sex outside of marriage, but to break the tension of these heavy topics we've been discussing and to give you some comic relief, I'll share a ridiculous, nonsexual true story about awkward nakedness from my own life. Feel free to have a good laugh at my expense.

NAKED AND EXPOSED

I was nervously fidgeting in a holding room wearing a hospital gown that covered almost nothing and was about to cover even less, given the exposure and nudity that would soon be required. The painkiller they'd given me beforehand was already taking effect, and, though my mind was still sharp, I could tell my body was starting to tingle with numbness. I would have rather been asleep altogether, because I'm a pretty modest person and I was about to assume a position that would make anyone blush.

I prayed two prayers in that waiting room. There's something about being in a hospital gown that makes you feel pretty powerless and reminds you to call on a higher power. The first prayer was that the procedure itself would go well and be painless. I wasn't too concerned about that part, so I spent more time on the second prayer.

The next prayer went something like this: "Lord, I'm about to be naked. You know that I wholeheartedly believe women can do things as well as men, oftentimes better than men. But today, I'd really appreciate it if no women were in this room. Other than my wife, I'd just rather not have a woman seeing me like this. And one more thing: please don't let me know any of the people in that room, and, if I can get really specific, I'd prefer to never run into them again after the procedure. I just would prefer not to see a guy at the grocery store and have to make small talk after they've seen me like this. Thanks, Lord. Amen."

I felt confident that God was going to take care of me on this prayer, but I was also feeling some regret that I hadn't driven to an out-of-town doctor's office for the procedure. They wheeled me into the room, and as I was contorted into an uncomfortable posture exposing more than I ever thought I'd be exposing in a well-lit public room, I looked around and saw there were only two men. I didn't recognize either of them. There wasn't a woman in sight.

Other than feeling like a bizarre, embarrassing dream, everything was going as well as could be expected. I took a deep breath and silently whispered a "thank you" prayer, but before I could finish it, an energetic female nurse burst into the room holding a clipboard and got a good look at my under-carriage before noticing my frightened face. When we made eye contact (which I was desperately trying to avoid) she nearly dropped her clipboard and exclaimed, "Pastor Dave! Oh my gosh! What are you doing here?"

I felt the answer to her question was obvious, so I opted not to answer. I'm not sure I would have had time to answer any-way, because she immediately continued. "Dave, you probably don't know me, but I'm Donna. I go to your church, and I love hearing your sermons, and your book *The Seven Laws of Love* is one of my all-time favorite books."

She then turned her attention to the men in the room and began a very effective sales pitch, trying to get them to read my blogs and books. If she ever quits her nursing job, she'd make an amazing promoter. I thought about trying to hire her to do publicity for this book, but I made a pact with myself never to contact her or make eye contact with her.

Donna said her goodbyes, and I managed to smile and wave from my awkward position. As the door closed behind her, I could hear her announce from the other side of the door, "Hey, girls. Pastor Dave is in there!"

I frantically looked around the room for a window or another exit I could use after the procedure, but, unfortu-nately, there was only one way out. When it was finished, I was wheeled out of the room to the waves and smiles from a throng of well-wishers, but it felt more like a gauntlet of paparazzi. I thought about changing my name and identity but, after looking into the complicated logistics of it, opted instead to just wear hats and sunglasses in public for a while.

Ashley and I had a good laugh in the waiting room afterward. I'm convinced even God had a good laugh at that one. I picture him smiling as I prayed and shaking his head, knowing what was about to happen. He might have called over an angel and said, "Hey, Gabriel. Get over here and watch what's about to happen to Dave! This is going to be hilarious!"

I share this silly story in a chapter about sex for a couple of reasons. First, it's funny, and you are entitled to some good laughs throughout this book! Second, even though there's nothing morally wrong about being seen naked during a medical procedure, it paints a picture of how we're not supposed to be comfortable with unrestricted nakedness around the opposite sex. I never want my boys to grow so calloused in sin that they trade "naked and unashamed" with their wife for "naked and shameless" with a long list of casual hookups. We should never feel uncomfortable being naked in front of our spouse, but we should never feel too comfortable being naked in front of anyone who is not our spouse.

CHILDLIKE INNOCENCE (AND NAKEDNESS)

As I write these words, I'm actually sitting in Chatham's bedroom helping him fall asleep. He's my youngest son at three years old, and he's going through a phase where he gets really scared at bedtime unless someone is with him. At first I saw his bedtime neediness as a huge hassle that prevented me from watching really important TV programs like reruns of *Seinfeld*, but now I actually look forward to bedtime. I get uninterrupted time with him, and then, while he's trying to fall asleep (which takes forever), I have some time to write.

I'm writing this tonight while he is gently humming along with a sound machine in his room playing lullabies on a loop. It's the most beautiful sound you can imagine. There's such a beautiful and unbridled innocence in childhood. It's an innocence that warms my heart.

When Chatham gets out of the bathtub at night and he's running through the house shaking his naked tail, he's truly naked and unashamed. I hope and pray that he, along with his big bros Cooper, Connor, and Chandler, will hold on to that beautiful innocence. I pray they'll keep childlike faith and add to it grown-up wisdom. I pray they change the world much more than the world changes them. I pray that even as grown-ups, within the beautiful covenant of marriage with wives they adore and respect, they'll be naked and unashamed.

In Women's Own Words

"I want my sons to know that sex isn't a game. The decisions you make about sex carry lifelong consequences. Society talks about 'safe sex,' but there's not a condom that can cover the human mind, heart, and soul."

—MAGGIE H. (AGE 45)

"If my dad knew the way boys at school talk around me, he'd seriously kill them. One creepy guy even got my cell number and texted me a picture of his penis. I was so grossed out! I deleted it right away and blocked the guy's number. If I ever told my parents, they'd freak out and call the police."

—KATE F. (AGE 15)

"When I was in college, I had sex with a guy after we had both been drinking quite a bit. He kept pushing me to do it, and I eventually went along with it, but if I had been sober, I know that there's no way I would have done it. I still feel such a mix of emotions over that night plus a lot of regret. I take responsibility for my actions, but I always wish he would have respected me enough . . . and respected himself enough . . . not to push for sex when we weren't thinking clearly."

—BARBARA K. (AGE 55)

"I'm a virgin, and I'm staying a virgin until my wedding night. Some of my friends think I'm a prude or living in the wrong century, but I know my future husband will be a man who respects me enough to support my decision and celebrate my values."

—SHELBY U. (AGE 20)

CHAPTER 6

THE PORN EPIDEMIC

*There is no dignity when the human dimen-
sion is eliminated from the person. In short,
the problem with pornography is not that
it shows too much of the person, but that it
shows far too little.*

—POPE JOHN PAUL II

If there's one force in our world that is causing more disrespect to women than any other, I would argue that force
would be pornography.

While a growing number of women are getting involved
with—and even addicted to—porn, it still remains largely an
exploitive form of entertainment produced by men and for

men. I'll share some stats and stories below to help illuminate why and how porn causes widespread disrespect to women, but first, let me share my own journey with porn. I know from experience that pornography can hijack a man's thinking and turn a respecter of women into a user of women.

My own struggle with pornography began as an adolescent curiosity. Nearly all boys are stimulated by visual images of females, and once the testosterone starts to kick in, the temptation to look and lust can become overwhelming. In my younger years, the options for lusting were limited. It was practically the dark ages when I was in middle school, so the Internet wasn't accessible. My first memories of intentional lust happened at Walmart. Yes, you heard me right: Walmart. I know, I know, it's sad.

Walmart had a section where you could look through posters. The posters were in frames and connected to some kind of rotating spine that allowed you to flip through them one at a time as if you were turning the pages on a giant book. The posters were mostly very innocent. There were posters of cartoons and baseball players and fast cars, but hidden away in the middle, there was always at least one poster of a girl in a bikini.

When we'd get to Walmart, I'd always tell Mom I wanted to go look around. I'd break loose from the family pack and make a beeline for the posters. I'd wait until nobody else was around, and then I'd go through the routine of pretending to look at all the posters, when really I was just fixating on the bikini girl.

My curiosity with women in bikinis quickly morphed into

a curiosity of women without bikinis. I had a friend who had some *Playboy* magazines under his bed. I remember the first time he handed me one. It felt like fire burning my hands. My heart was racing. I knew it was wrong to lust after women, but all the willpower I could summon wasn't nearly enough to keep me from opening up that centerfold. Once I saw those airbrushed images, I was hooked, but being "hooked" on porn doesn't mean you want more of the same thing. It means you always need something different.

The next step in my digression came when one of my friends got ahold of some hardcore porn magazines. Once I saw those graphic images, looking wasn't enough anymore. I had to have a physical release while I looked. Those magazines pierced me with the double-edged sword of porn and masturbation. I'd look, and then I'd fantasize, and then I'd masturbate.

The magazines paved the way to movies, and by this time, Internet access to porn made every fantasy just a click away. My brain was being rewired to see women as sexual objects there for my on-demand access, to use and discard at my disposal. I was losing control. Even when I was able to go stretches of time without looking at porn, I'd still replay those images in my mind and masturbate daily. It was an addictive cycle, and I wasn't sure I'd ever break free.

I justified in my mind that I wasn't really using anyone, since these were merely images on a screen or in a magazine. This was just entertainment. Nobody was getting hurt. I believed that lie for a while, until I noticed that I could no longer look at an attractive woman without undressing her in my mind and fantasizing about her performing sex acts at my command.

My mind became a warped place. I would still have said I respected women, but a more honest statement would have been that I wanted to respect women. My lustful sins had sabotaged my good intentions, and I'd lost control.

By sheer willpower, I'd stay away from porn for weeks or even months at a time, but I'd always fall back into that same dark pit, because I never sought accountability. I never followed the biblical roadmap for healing, which always involves repentance. I followed the path of pride, and pride tells you that nobody needs to know and you can take care of things on your own.

I carried my porn secret into my marriage without telling Ashley it had been a past struggle. I thought I had been "cured" of it, and I also believed the myth that once I was married and had a healthy outlet for my sex drive, I'd never be tempted by porn again. I turned out to be very wrong, and I fell back into that same dark pit about a year into our marriage.

When Ashley found the sites I'd visited on our computer, I was heartbroken, ashamed, and relieved all at once. We started a journey toward healing, and I'm so thankful she responded with grace. Even though she was deeply wounded by my dishonesty and my lustful sin, she chose to forgive and offered me the opportunity to rebuild the trust I'd broken.

I'm so thankful for God's grace and my wife's grace. I don't know where I'd be without them!

I'm happy to report that I've been free from porn for years now. While it seems like a distant memory, I still have to battle against the dark images embedded in my mind and still find myself having to pry my eyes away from seductive images all around me. It's an ongoing battle for me and for most men of all ages.

Every stat I've seen says that the majority of men and teenage boys have a current struggle with porn. I see that familiar look in the eyes of so many. It's a look I used to have and I still battle against. It's a look of scanning the horizon for any woman to "check out." It's a look that objectifies, mentally undresses, and uses women instead of respecting them.

We can't expect our words of respect to be believed when our eyes are telling a different story. We must be a generation that agrees with Jesus that lust is sin. Porn is immeasurably harmful to both the actors who make it and the billions of consumers who watch it.

If we are to teach our boys to respect girls, we need to have some important conversations with them about porn.

WHAT EVERY PARENT NEEDS TO KNOW ABOUT PORN

"It seems so obvious: If we invent a machine, the first thing we are going to do—after making a profit—is use it to watch porn. When the projector was invented roughly a century ago, the first movies were not of damsels in distress tied to train tracks or Charlie Chaplin–style slapsticks; they were stilted porn shorts called stag films. VHS became the dominant standard for VCRs largely because

Sony wouldn't allow pornographers to use Betamax; the movie industry followed porn's lead. DVDs, the Internet, cell phones. You name it, pornography planted its big flag there first, or at least shortly thereafter."

—DAMON BROWN, AUTHOR OF *PORN AND PONG* AND *PLAYBOY'S GREATEST COVERS*[1]

"This material is more aggressive, more harmful, more violent, more degrading and damaging than at any other time in the history of the world. And this generation growing up is dealing with it to an intensity and scale no other generation in the history of the world has ever had to."

—CLAY OLSEN, COFOUNDER AND CEO OF FIGHT THE NEW DRUG[2]

I recently read an article where a researcher gathered a focus group of high school students together to ask about their exposure to pornography and their thoughts related to porn. The kids didn't know it at the time, but the parents of these mostly middle-class teenagers, ages fourteen to sixteen years old, were watching the conversation on a live video in a different room. The parents quickly became shocked and appalled by what their kids were saying.

"Have you ever seen a 'nugget'?" one of the boys asked while laughing. The rest of the kids laughed and chimed in, saying things like, "Oh, yeah! I'd totally get with a 'nugget,' because she'd have to do whatever you wanted." The researcher wasn't even sure what "nugget" referred to, and the kids told him it's a porn term to refer to a woman with no arms and no legs who performs sex acts in porn movies. Not only did all these kids know the term; most of them had apparently seen this type of porn and described it in vivid detail.

The researcher asked about their first exposures to porn and how they had access to it. Most of them had seen pornography before their eleventh birthdays, and most of them—boys and girls—now looked at porn with at least some regularity. A few of the boys appeared to already be addicted. When asked how they got access to porn, the kids began pulling out smartphones and showing apps that looked innocent (app icons that looked like calculators or games or other "innocent" things) but were actually designed to hide videos, pictures, and any-thing else the kids didn't want their parents to see. Even if their phones got taken away, the kids talked about how they could see whatever they wanted on their friends' phones.

The conversation continued when the researcher changed the subject and asked what words came to their minds when they thought about porn. The first word someone threw out was "anal," followed by "oral," and slang terms referring to oral and anal sex. All the other kids started agreeing, saying that porn sex always included oral and anal sex as well as vaginal intercourse.

The researcher asked how pornography had shaped their views and expectations of sex. One girl spoke up and said, "Boys always expect you to have 'porn sex.'" Another girl spoke up and talked about how women in porn never had pubic hair, so now boys are grossed out by any pubic hair. One boy laughed and said, "They're gorillas!" apparently referring to any woman with unshaved pubic hair.

As the conversation continued, it became apparent that even if these kids were exaggerating their own experiences to impress their peers, the stats suggested that their experience was much more common than we'd like to admit. Kids' exposure to porn (and adults' exposure to porn as well) is having a massive impact on individuals, relationships, and society as a whole. The data is staggering.

We need to have some very honest conversations with our kids, and we need to teach them about porn and sex. If we're not willing to have these conversations, trust me, there are plenty of their friends who will be happy to have these conversations with them instead. To equip ourselves for these conversations, let's look at six important facts every parent needs to know about porn.

1. The average age of first exposure to pornography is eleven years old. By the time a child has graduated from high school, 95 percent of kids have been exposed to porn, whether they were looking for it or not.[3]

These sobering stats are a reminder that we need to do everything in our power to protect our kids from being exposed to porn early. Exposure will most likely happen at some point no matter what we do, but we still need to do everything in our power to guard their eyes and their hearts. Porn fuels lust, and lust fuels disrespect. Porn is perhaps the most universal link shared by all men who disrespect women. When lust goes unchecked and porn use intensifies, a young boy's mind can scarcely think of a woman without mentally objectifying and disrespecting her. I know this from research, but I also know this from personal experience. Porn producers are aggressively pushing their smut to turn our kids into addicted porn consumers, and parents must be fanatical in the fight against porn. Some tools help you block porn and monitor all Internet activity. A few great resources to help you are Circle, which is an Internet filtering device from Disney, as well as porn-blocking software like Covenant Eyes or X3Watch.[4] Also, as I mentioned earlier, one of the best resources for helping you have honest conversations about healthy sexuality is Passport2Purity from Family Life Today.

2. The actors in porn films perpetuate a fantasy, but they're often in physical pain.

Carlo Scalisi, the owner of a pornographic production company, was quoted as saying, "Amateurs come across better on screen. Our customers feel that. You can see it in the women's faces that they're experiencing pain and that's a turn on to many of our viewers."[5] Let that thought sink in. Much of the porn industry is intentionally serving up graphic, violent content objectifying women and cultivating a twisted version of pleasure brought on by seeing a woman suffering. I'm not sure how any reasonable person could think there's no link between the porn industry and our world's widespread mistreatment of women. Intentionally causing a woman pain or deriving pleasure from her pain is a grotesque form of disrespect.

The long-term effect on porn actors and porn consumers can lead to sexual dysfunction and emotional dysfunction in future relationships and marriages. In a world designed to create pleasure, there's much pain happening behind the scenes. There's pain and often abuse in the backgrounds of the performers, and there will be future pain in the relationships of all who drink from the poisoned well of pornography.[6]

3. Porn has the same impact on your brain as an addictive drug.

The porn industry makes more money than all professional sports combined, and because a lot of money is at stake, people don't want to admit that porn is destructive or addictive, but it is! Porn use is linked to depression, anxiety, sexism, sex crimes, divorce, and countless other physical, emotional, and relationship issues. The website www.FightTheNewDrug.org contains compelling scientific evidence showing that ongoing exposure to porn has the same negative effect on the mind as a heroin addiction.[7]

4. Porn is the enemy of love.

I wholeheartedly believe this is true on a number of levels. As a Christian, I can give you plenty of Bible verses—including Jesus saying that to look at a woman lustfully is to commit adultery in your heart, and countless other passages about love, sex, and marriage—but even if you don't share my faith, the stats alone should be enough to make you want to stay away from porn for the rest of your life. It ruins marriages. It sabotages love. It is a primary source of disrespect toward women. It creates the illusion of connection, but it's a manufacturer of disparities and divisions between men and women.

It rewires the brain in devastating ways. It leads to widespread relational dysfunction and can desensitize the users from being able to experience sexual and/or emotional intimacy in later relationships.[8]

5. Most kids don't see porn as wrong.

A recent study revealed that 96 percent of teenagers and young adults were either accepting or neutral when it came to their opinion of pornography. Only 4 percent believed it was wrong or a sin. This moral indifference is fueling massive consumption of porn. In 2016 on one website alone, consumers watched 4.6 billion hours of porn. That's the equivalent of seventeen thousand entire lifetimes, and it happened all in one year and all on one website.[9]

6. Porn and other cybersex-related activities can be as damaging to a marriage as an actual, physical affair.

In an in-depth project by researcher Jennifer P. Schneider, survey data measured the long-term impact of porn and other cybersex activities, which includes sexting and sharing sexually explicit images online. The research indicated that this activity is incredibly damaging to relationships, and those married indicated that the aftermath of these online activities can be every bit as painful as an actual physical affair. This is particularly harmful, since most people don't see these online activities as a form of infidelity or even as being wrong.[10] Separate research has also found that the divorce rate for couples who view pornography is nearly twice as high as the divorce rate for couples who don't view porn.[11]

TEACHING OUR SONS THE BENEFITS AND POTENTIAL PITFALLS OF TECHNOLOGY

"Of the thousands of incarcerated sex offenders and Sexually Violent Predators I worked with over the course of 11+ years, not one of them would have believed they would have ended up offending. They simply played on the edge, harmonized with darkness, & saturated themselves in porn."

—JON K. UHLER[12]

My sons are better with technology than I am. Their generation has been dubbed "Digital Natives," which means technology is like a native language for them. They were born with access to smartphones. They're learning how to code in middle school. They have the world's knowledge literally at their fingertips, and they are already shaping the world's future through their technological prowess.

As we talk to our kids about respect for women and porn and sex, we also need to talk to them about the good use and the misuse of technology. We can neither demonize nor deify technology. We must teach our boys responsible principles to help them navigate the opportunities and potential pitfalls related to the incredible tech they hold in their hands.

For all the good technology has brought into our kids' world, it has also opened them up to some terrible images. Tech can also provide a dangerous illusion of consequence-free interactions with others. Many video games and other online platforms let kids create pseudo-identities through avatars that can insult, violate, or even kill others without restraint or punishment. Many people will argue that these online games and interactions are harmless, but I theorize that nearly all real-life acts of violence and disrespect toward women were first acted out online before it ever happened in the real world.

I don't want to be like my legalistic great-grandmother who used to call the television "the Devil's Box" and reprimand my great-grandfather for watching Walter Cronkite or college basketball on the small black-and-white screen. There's a temptation to demonize technology, because it's easier to condemn something than to wade into the murky mess of learning it, explaining it, and leveraging it for good. As followers of Christ, we have a God-given mandate to leverage technology for good and for building the kingdom, but we must first teach our kids principles that will help them use it wisely and understand the hard truths that there are many people using it for wretched purposes.

Recently, in a horrifying misuse of technology and exploitation of girls, Facebook unknowingly became the facilitator of a slave auction. A father auctioned his sixteen-year-old daughter off in marriage to the highest bidder in a post originating in South Sudan. The label of "marriage" was a thinly veiled disguise attempting to mask sex trafficking as something more noble. Most teenage brides are sold off to much older men, and many of those men already have multiple wives.

When Facebook learned of this nefarious use of their technology, they removed the post. It proved to be too late. The father had sold his daughter to a rapist in exchange for some cows, cars, and cash. Similar auctions happen online and in less sophisticated ways millions of times per year.[13]

Our kids need to be a light in the darkness in their schools, in their relationships, and even on the Internet, but we must also be careful not to send them out into the darkness too soon, unsupervised, or unprepared. We must have healthy ongoing conversations to make sure we're giving them the guidance, accountability, and protection they'll need. We need to teach them mastery of technology, but we also need to protect them from the dangers technology can create, like the on-demand access to pornography and countless other nefarious misuses of tech. Our sons must also be reminded that the disrespect or objectification of women in a virtual setting is never acceptable or inconsequential.

There's not a magic formula to help parents get the tech talk right every time. It all comes down to the themes that are at the heart of this entire book: communication, integrity, and respect. Model these principles for your son, and be vigilant and involved with him every step of the way. You'll be on the right track, and you'll earn the trust and credibility to be a continuing influence in his life long after he's grown and gone from under your roof.

Here are a few of my favorite tips and tools related to teaching your sons to be wise, savvy, and safe when it comes to technology:

1. **Monitor their web activities.** Your son doesn't have a right to privacy on the Internet while he is a minor living in your home. Check his activity often. If you're

unsure how to accurately check search history and online activity, then ask a tech-savvy friend or associate to periodically check your devices for you.

2. **Let your son know that he's being monitored.** Have a secret-free policy on all his Internet activity. Add the extra accountability measures of porn-blocking software and web-tracking apps. These resources are constantly changing, but a few apps and tools that have been helpful around our house to keep us all accountable have been the ones mentioned earlier: X3Watch, Covenant Eyes, and Circle by Disney as well as Bark.us.

3. **Limit screen time.** Our boys would play video games 24-7 if we allowed it. We've learned to leverage screen time as a reward and remove it as a punishment. We've also blocked off most weekdays as a time when video games are off-limits.

4. **Encourage positive and innovative tech usage.** We want our boys to be great with tech so that they can do great things with technology. Ashley and I have been able to reach millions of people around the world with a positive message—all because of technology. We share our online work with our kids and encourage them to do the same with us. Our older boys are already better with technology than we are! They're launching YouTube channels and other positive (and possibly profitable) tech-based endeavors. Of course, these activities require increased vigilance on our part, but it's a small price to pay to prepare our kids

to be good stewards of the powerful gift of technology they'll have at their fingertips all their lives.

SEX ROBOTS AND THE FUTURE OF TECH-BASED LUST

We live in an era where technology is advancing at a dizzying speed. Many of the innovators on the forefront of these technological advancements are sadly those who are peddling pornography and other tech-based forms of sexual entertainment. The latest craze in the tech-sex boom follows the growing demand for sex robots.

A recent local news story reported that my home state of Texas is set to open its first "brothel" made up of high-tech sex robots. I watched in amazement as the anchors seamlessly transitioned from local weather and sports to featuring creepily lifelike robots equipped with artificial intelligence who are designed to respond to the sexual commands and preferences of their male customers. The news story became a sort of advertisement for the brothel by giving the hourly rates for rental and the sale prices for those customers who wanted their own on-demand robotic sex slave in the comfort of their own home.[14]

The story featured interviews with concerned residents who thought the whole concept was seedy and creepy, but those profiting from the new boom in sex robots argued that it's simply meeting a service. It's simply supply and demand. Beyond the pure capitalism of it, there are no actual victims.

It's essentially a high-tech form of masturbation. Many argued that the on-demand option for sexual gratification will lower the demand for sex trafficking and instances of sexual assault. These arguments are clearly wrong and are perpetuated only by those with selfish motives.

As I pondered the future of how technology will facilitate sexual sin for profit, I had several initial thoughts. First, I noticed that all these sex robots were designed to look like young women barely eighteen years of age. Some of them appeared to look like girls even younger than the legal age of consent. Troubling. My mind also flashed back to all the Old Testament warnings against bestiality, which is essentially using any nonhuman body for sexual gratification. God's Word has always given clear warning about the misuse of sex in any form.

For all the Old Testament parallels and the creepy grossness of the entire concept, what troubles me the most has to do with the disrespect toward women that will undoubtedly be ignited by this practice. You might argue that it's impossible to show disrespect to women by how you treat a robot. I'd argue that it matters how you treat the image of a woman, and that it significantly impacts how you treat women in general. In fact, I'd argue that it matters a lot.

The human mind is a training ground for our beliefs, and our beliefs become our actions. If a child practices loving and nurturing a baby doll, the child will most likely love and nurture a real-life baby sibling in a similar way. If an adult uses and objectifies a doll made in the image of a woman, his mind will eventually justify the objectification of actual women.

RAISING BOYS WHO RESPECT GIRLS

His mind will be rewired to see sex as a selfish act where it's impossible to abuse a sexual partner, because like his robots, she exists only for his own sexual pleasure. Her pleasure (or even her consent) is not a consequential matter as long as he gets what he wants. If you regularly have sex with an object that you own, it won't be long before you treat a human sexual partner like an object that you own.

> IT MATTERS HOW YOU TREAT THE IMAGE OF A WOMAN; IT SIGNIFICANTLY IMPACTS HOW YOU TREAT WOMEN IN GENERAL.

Perhaps you believe I'm making quite a stretch to argue that those who look at porn or those who partake in sexual forms of entertainment are all sexists. I'm not trying to paint with broad strokes in judging or labeling people, but I am trying to plead to our collective reason. The sexual entertainment industry is poisoning our minds and, consequently, poisoning our relationships. Until we can admit that what happens in the mind matters, then we're setting ourselves—and our sons—up for some terrible choices.

As a man who struggled with porn in my teenage years and into early adulthood, I can personally testify to the negative impacts porn can have on a person and on a marriage. Now that my wife and I work with married couples, every day we see marriages crumbling because of porn use. Please teach your kids that porn destroys. Be honest about your own experiences and mistakes. Ask them questions and be a safe place for them to process all they're thinking, feeling, and struggling

128

with. Don't let somebody else have these conversations for you. Too much is at stake!

Teach your sons to stay away from porn, and stay away from it in your own life too. Porn sabotages our thinking. It turns respecters of women into users and even abusers of women. It might seem easy to justify viewing porn as a harmless form of sexual exploration, but watching porn as a means of meeting your sexual needs is like drinking poison as a means of quenching your thirst. It might seem to satisfy in the moment, but it will always hurt you in the end.

In Women's Own Words

"My husband talked me into watching porn with him. I was grossed out at first, but then, to be honest, it made our sex life better for a while. At least, I thought it was helping. It added something exciting, but later I realized it was really poisoning our relationship. We started drifting apart outside the bedroom, and eventually, my husband had an affair. We're actually divorced now, and I honestly trace all our problems back to that decision to bring porn into our marriage. I wish we never would have done it. I honestly believe we'd still be married."

—DANA K. (AGE 39)

"Almost all the guys at my college look at porn. They talk about it all the time like you'd talk about watching cartoons or something. They act like it's no big deal, but the way they look at women and the way they talk about women . . . you can tell porn is poisoning their minds. I once had a guy tell me that I looked just like a girl in his favorite porno and then he looked me up and down like he was undressing me in his mind. I think it was supposed to be a compliment or something, but I've seriously never been so grossed out in my life! It's sad. I want to marry a guy who is not into porn. I don't want to compete with that garbage."

—STACY L. (AGE 21)

"I thought I was doing everything right to protect my sons from porn, but I found the search history on our home computer and I realized our fourteen-year-old son is already hooked on it. I feel like I've failed as a mom. I wish porn didn't exist."

—MARCY R. (AGE 38)

CHAPTER 7

LUST AND MASTURBATION

*I say, anyone who even looks at a woman with
lust has already committed adultery with her
in his heart.*

—JESUS (MATTHEW 5:28)

I f you have a teenage son, there's a good chance he's masturbating more often than he's brushing his teeth. Seriously.

I don't share this secret of adolescent males with you to
disgust you or shock you. I simply want you to be aware that
almost all boys masturbate and do it very often from early adolescence through early adulthood. You might be wondering

RAISING BOYS WHO RESPECT GIRLS

what a teenage boy's shower habits have to do with respecting girls, and you might also be wondering why there's an entire chapter focused specifically on this subject.

The answer is this: the rampant masturbation most boys experience through adolescence is training their minds and their bodies to view women and girls as sexualized objects and on-demand fantasies for their own sexual gratification. It can become a selfish, tangible manifestation of disrespect toward women. I know this from research, but I also know this from personal experience. Here are some eye-opening confessions of teen boys paraphrased from research, social media submissions, and interviews:

> "I want to respect girls, and sometimes I feel like I do, but I have masturbated fantasizing about almost every pretty girl I know. It's hard for me to see a girl or think about a girl or talk to a girl without immediately thinking about sex. I'm afraid that if girls knew what was actually happening in my mind, they'd run away screaming and never want to talk to me again."
>
> —JACKSON (AGE 16)

> "When I'm talking to another guy, I always look him in the eyes, but I've noticed that when I talk to girls, I always look at their mouths when they're talking. Instead of hearing what they're saying, I'm fantasizing about kissing them; or worse, I'm fantasizing about them giving me oral sex. I've watched so much oral sex in porn that now my brain sees a girl's mouth as a sex organ. It's what I think about when

I masturbate. I can't even have a conversation with a girl without thinking about it."

—BLAKE (AGE 18)

"The first time I masturbated, I felt dirty and guilty . . . but I also felt really good. The more I did it, the less dirty I felt, but it still feels good every time. Sometimes I'll get so turned on watching the cheerleaders practice during gym class that I'll run to the locker room pretending to be using the bathroom, but really I'm thinking about the cheerleaders and masturbating. I'd die if I ever got caught doing that at school!"

—LUKE (AGE 15)

As for my own story . . . actually, let me make a quick personal announcement. My mom reads everything I write, because she's a loving, supportive, encouraging, wonderful mother. Mom, I know you're reading this right now, but please skip the rest of this chapter. It's already awkward to admit what I'm about to admit, and it will be much more awkward knowing you're reading it! I love you. Now, please skip ahead. If you don't skip ahead, I might not ever be able to make eye contact with you again without blushing.

Okay, where was I? As for my own story, over the course of my teenage years, I masturbated literally thousands of times. I'd estimate I averaged one or two times per day for a solid decade. It was as much a part of my life as eating food, and much like food, I felt I was going to die from starvation if I went long without doing it. That was awkward to admit, and just to give you fair warning, this conversation is probably going to get even more awkward. Stay with me as I share some intimate details from my past. This has an important point.

The early triggers to masturbate could be anything from seeing a lingerie ad on TV to seeing a girl in tight shorts walk by. I didn't have access to porn in those early adolescent years, but I did have a postcard hidden in my underwear drawer. I'd bought the postcard at a souvenir shop on a family trip to Myrtle Beach, and it had a titillating picture of a woman wearing a wet T-shirt that left little to the imagination. That fifty-cent postcard was like a gateway drug eventually leading me to more graphic forms of pornography.

My masturbation habit was fed by porn, and the more I consumed porn, the more voracious appetite I had for masturbation. The more often I masturbated, the higher my sex drive became and the more porn I wanted to consume, so one sin fed the other in a vicious cycle that felt inescapable at the time. The twin sins of porn and masturbation are so intricately connected, but of the two, masturbation was the more difficult to quit. Even after I finally broke free from pornography, it took me several more years to completely stop masturbating.

The irony about this cycle of pleasure-seeking sin is that I found so little pleasure in it. Whenever we give ourselves over to any sin, there's a numbness that begins to settle into our souls as a spiritual form of gangrene eats away at our inner selves. I was chasing pleasure, but I found little. I was a self-loathing fool, searching for fleeting moments of bliss instead of the steadfast presence of true joy and peace.

Like Esau in the Old Testament, I was trading my

God-given blessings to sinfully satisfy a momentary hunger. With each of my returns to this sin, I found less pleasure and more misery. Despite the diminishing returns of my actions, I proceeded with the desperation of an addict and the hopelessness of a fool. Once I finally came to my senses and committed to embracing God's grace and following God's plan, it was still a long journey until I found complete healing and deliverance.

Once I finally broke free from pornography, I realized that my brain had been rewired to play highlight reels of porn on a loop in my head. My thoughts were perpetually haunted, and, during the period of detox, masturbation became like a form of methadone, which is what helps drug addicts wean off a drug while their bodies are going through detox. Masturbation was my methadone. Even though I wasn't watching porn, I was still infected. My mind and body had become interconnected in an intricate web of sin resulting from years of lust.

Even all these years later, I still get flashbacks of my old, toxic thought life when certain images sneak into my brain through billboards or TV ads or unexpected steamy scenes on TV. It's a lifelong struggle, and staying away from porn and masturbation is like a form of sobriety. I've never been addicted to a substance, but in retrospect, I now recognize I was fully addicted and enslaved to these sins. Staying free from them still requires constant vigilance and intentionality.

If you're a woman reading this, you might be shocked by this or even assume my experience was abnormal. While some women have had experiences that mirror my own in these areas, this tends to disproportionately affect men. Most men reading this are probably nodding their heads in agreement, because their experiences were likely similar to mine. Back in my school days, my buddies and I would talk openly about masturbation, and we even once had an informal contest to see who could masturbate the most in a month. I lost, and assuming he was telling the truth, the guy who won almost doubled my total.

As a very important point of clarification, just because masturbation is "normal," in that almost all boys do it, it doesn't make its rampant presence right. Even while I was caught up in the endless cycle of lust and self-gratification through masturbation, I knew it was wrong. I knew Jesus had taught about lust being a form of adultery, and I knew what the Bible had to say about not even having a hint of sexual immorality. Still, I found it easy to justify my "minor sin" in light of the alternatives. I'd think justifying thoughts like,

> Well, I'm not having sex with anyone, so nobody is getting hurt.
> It's my body, and I'm just doing routine maintenance.
> There are a lot worse things I could be doing. This is probably even healthy.
> One day, I'll have a wife and I won't need to do this, and in the meantime, this is just something that has to be done.

Of course, all my justifications were shallow lies meant to help me feel better about my sin. I thought I was in control, but I wasn't. I thought I could keep the sins of masturbation and lust locked neatly in a compartment of my mind and my life that would never really impact my relationships. I was wrong.

After a while, porn and masturbation weren't enough to satisfy. It led me to a world of compromises I never thought I'd make. I went into college having only kissed one girl and swearing to myself that, beyond my sin with lust and masturbation, I would never cross any sexual boundaries with a woman. I would remain completely "pure" until marriage. I was blind to my hypocrisy. My thought life was vulgar and X-rated and I'd play those mental images on repeat, but I still convinced myself the sin was under control. I even commended myself for my sexual restraint. I was a fool.

Within the first few months of college, I'd started a dating relationship with a young woman and pretty quickly allowed our relationship to escalate physically beyond my preset boundaries. It started with heavy petting, but I soon crossed the line into mutual masturbation. I reasoned, "Hey, if I'm going to be masturbating anyway, then what's the harm of having someone do it for me?"

My girlfriend was a nice person, but I knew I wasn't going to marry her. Staying in the relationship and continuing the sin was an intimate form of disrespect. I was using her for my own pleasure. I justified it by reasoning that we weren't actually having sex, so it wasn't a big deal, but I knew it was wrong. I just didn't care enough to quit. I allowed my conscience to be numbed so my pleasure could be heightened, and it proved to be a very damaging trade-off.

Even after that relationship ended and I had an opportunity for a fresh start, I found myself slipping into a dark season of sin and compromise. I had several casual encounters and one brief relationship where I continued to push the boundaries and started justifying oral sex. Even though Bill Clinton had recently argued on national television that oral sex wasn't really sex, I knew I'd crossed another massive line. I knew that the loopholes I was trying to create to justify my technical virginity weren't impressing God. Biblical truth always trumps popular opinion.

Thankfully, I came to my senses and repented, which is a churchy way of saying I decided to have a fresh start and head in a new direction. God's grace was there to guide the way. By the time I met Ashley on the first day of my junior year, I was in a better place in my faith than I had been in a long time. I wanted to be a man of integrity and genuine faith who was worthy of her respect.

When we started dating, we committed to sexual purity, and we didn't cross any of those boundaries we had established. Our wedding night was the first time either of us had intercourse, which was such a special gift we were able to give each other. I'm so thankful for the choice we made to honor God in our relationship, but I still carry regret over the compromises I made and the sins I justified before Ashley and I met. I wish I could go back in time and tell my younger self this: never trade temporary pleasure for permanent regret.

A few years after we were married, I relapsed into the cycle of porn and masturbation. The waves of shame and disgust I felt as I fell back into this pit of sin were overwhelming. God's grace and Ashley's grace, plus some much-needed accountability, helped me break the cycle once and for all, but it still devastates me to know the pain I caused my precious wife because of my selfish sin.

When I think back to the pain I've caused Ashley and the disrespect I've displayed toward other women, it motivates me to implement something I refer to as Retroactive Respect. I can't build a time machine to travel back and undo my past sins, but I can do something proactive that honors the women in my past, present, and future. I can look for daily opportunities to learn from the past and choose to be more intentional in showing respect every day. I can also teach these lessons to my sons, and you can do the same with yours. It might require some uncomfortable confessions on your part, like the ones I've just shared with you, but do whatever is necessary to help your sons make wise choices, especially when it relates to sexual purity. Teach them that sins like lust and masturbation, which seem so easy to justify, will always lead to more destructive sins if they're allowed to continue. No sin is harmless.

Sin never stays in the compartment you build for it. The sexual fantasies you play on repeat in your brain can't stay in your mind forever without impacting other aspects of your life. The Bible tells us that as a person thinks in his heart, so is he (Prov. 23:7). In other words, our thought life will shape our real life. Our thoughts create the road map of our lives and our relationships. Everything we ever do, good or bad, begins in the mind long before it's acted out.

When the apostle Paul encouraged the Philippian church to "think about things that are excellent and worthy of praise" (Phil. 4:8), he was

> EVERYTHING WE EVER DO, GOOD OR BAD, BEGINS IN THE MIND LONG BEFORE IT'S ACTED OUT.

talking about much more than the power of positive thinking. He was reminding them—and us—that the frontlines of spiritual warfare exist between our ears. The brain is the most powerful sex organ of all.

THE MIND: THE MOST POWERFUL HUMAN SEX ORGAN

As I was reading, researching, soul-searching, and praying about what needed to be included in this book, I quickly realized that I needed to not just focus on what boys were doing with their penises but I also needed to focus on what's happening in their minds. Respect or disrespect toward women begins with thoughts. Sexual restraint or sexual sin begins in the mind. Breaking bad habits and starting healthy habits all begins in the mind. The more we can understand what boys are thinking and feeling, the more we'll be able to help them make wise and healthy choices.

I'm not a psychologist or a neuroscientist, so I knew I'd need some backup on this aspect of the book. Part of my research included an interview with my good friend Shaunti Feldhahn, who is a bestselling author and a brilliant researcher on issues related to human relationships. She and her husband, Jeff, are both cited in this book, and their research and insights have helped me tremendously.

Shaunti shared with me some brilliant and thought-provoking insights about differences in the male thought process and the female thought process and how these differences impact boys' behavior. She shared cutting-edge neurological research that showed differences in male brain scans versus female brain scans when people were shown images of an attractive person of the opposite sex. Completely different parts of the brain would light up on the scan for each gender.

I'll summarize Shaunti's insights in layperson's terms, but you can get the full scope of her groundbreaking research in her book coauthored with my friend Craig Gross. It's called *Through a Man's Eyes: Helping Women Understand the Visual Nature of Men.*[1]

Shaunti explained that while men and women both find pleasure in looking at an attractive person of the opposite sex, and both genders can be tempted by visual lust or pornography, there are some major differences. A woman's brain lights up in the prefrontal cortex, which is sort of the Grand Central Station of the brain. From there, she remains in control of what she chooses to do with those images. She can choose to dwell on them or discard them, but the process is logical and she typically feels empowered to do what she wishes with those mental images.

For men and boys, the process is completely different. When the image of an attractive woman or any sexualized image enters his brain, it doesn't start at the prefrontal cortex. It lights up the base of his brain, which triggers a more primal reaction, and it can feel like mental warfare for him to try to wrench those images or thoughts out of his mind before they start playing on a sexualized highlight reel in his brain.

This process may be different for men, but this doesn't

mean men are powerless against their thought lives. It simply means men will usually have to be more vigilant against sexualized imagery and more intentional about renewing their minds. As Martin Luther said, "You can't keep a bird from flying over your head, but you can keep it from building a nest in your hair."

Luther was talking about our thought lives. We can't always control which thoughts or images shoot through our brains, but even though it might cause temptation, we get to choose which thoughts and images we allow to dwell there.

Max Lucado shared a similar analogy in his bestselling book *Anxious for Nothing*. He gave the analogy of your mind being an airport and the airplanes representing all the different thoughts, images, and worries that are coming and going at all times. He challenged the reader to realize we hold the power as the air traffic controller of our minds. We ultimately determine which thoughts "land" and which ones fly away.[2]

God has indeed given us great power in our minds, and in his wisdom, he also created unique differences in how men and women process things. While these differences are ultimately a good thing, they can create unintentional disrespect and miscommunication when males and females are unaware these differences exist.

Some misconceptions relate directly to the different ways males and females process images of the opposite sex. In his book *For Young Men Only*, Jeff Feldhahn conducted hundreds of interviews with teen boys and teen girls. He found that when girls dressed in tight clothes, most boys assumed that they were intentionally doing so to invite sexual advances or to induce sexual fantasies in the boys who saw them. The boys assumed that the girls knew that boys would look at any bare skin or tight clothes in sexualized terms, and, therefore, the girls must want to be viewed through a sexualized lens.

When Jeff interviewed girls about this same topic, most girls were horrified and shocked that boys would think this way. The majority of girls said they chose their clothes based primarily on what was in fashion, and it never occurred to them that boys would view them or their clothing in a sexual way. Most girls were repulsed by the idea of boys thinking of them as objects of lust during masturbation. In fact, only 4 percent of girls reported choosing their clothes with a motive of getting sexual attention from boys, while 90 percent of boys thought the girls were dressing to get sexual attention. This is one of many examples of how misperceptions can cause unintentional tension and disrespect.[3]

Just to be clear, it's inappropriate for a boy to objectify a girl regardless of what she's wearing, even if she's among the 4 percent dressing provocatively as an intentional attempt to gain sexual attention. I'm not going to dive into the minefield of debate on how girls should dress or what they should be doing differently to create healthy dynamics in coed relationships. Those are subjects for another book by another author. The one bit of commentary I will share is that most girls and women would think about their wardrobes in a different way if they fully knew what was happening in the male brain.

Males might be hardwired with a visual temptation to lust, but while temptation might be inevitable, lust is always optional. In *Through a Man's Eyes* Shaunti summarized this concept well by stating, "Although neuroscience shows that the first reaction is instinctive and biological rather than voluntary, the next step is always a choice."[4]

Much of the lust, miscommunication, and unintentional messages being sent from boys to girls and vice versa result from unclear standards or unspoken questions. What can we do as parents to provide clarity? We need to understand the reality of the situation. First, boys are fighting raging hormones, constant visual temptation, and mental warfare over how they should be responding. Second, most boys have the misconception that girls want to be the objects of their sexual fantasies or sexual attention simply because of how they dress. Third, boys need to know it's never appropriate or respectful to sexualize or objectify any girl for any reason, regardless of what the girl is wearing.

Our boys also need to know that they can win this battle. They must win this battle. They can't make excuses. They must also know that you, as a mom or dad, are a safe place for them to ask questions. I know these conversations can be awkward and messy and scary, but that's part of being a parent. Be a safe place for your son.

Most of our boys secretly feel powerless over their sexual thoughts, and the thought of waiting until marriage to have any healthy outlet for their sexual energy seems impossible. One of our most important tasks as parents is to help them find the courage, strength, and belief that God has given them the power to do what feels impossible. They need to be reminded that they can do all things through Christ who gives them strength (Phil. 4:13).

THE POWER TO DO
DIFFICULT THINGS

Ashley recently purchased an online video conference for our older sons. The conference is called "Do Hard Things," and it is taught by twin brothers Alex and Brett Harris who were still teenagers themselves at the time the video was recorded. These high-achieving brothers also wrote a bestselling book of the same title.[5]

Our sons Cooper and Connor moaned and complained when we fired up the laptop and started the videos. They would have much rather been playing Fortnite, but we told them that these videos were worthwhile. Within a few minutes of the teaching, my boys had stopped fidgeting and complaining and were captivated by what they were learning.

In the video, the teenaged twins were sharing to a packed auditorium of thousands of other adolescents. The brothers talked about our culture's low expectations for teens, and how these low expectations of delayed adulthood were a stark contrast to the expectations of previous generations. They shared inspiring stories of young men and women from the past who had led great movements in their teenage years and then challenged those watching to do the same. Instead of rebelling against rules or their parents, the teens were challenged to rebel against a culture of entitlement, apathy, and laziness.

I was fighting the urge to stand up and cheer, but I maintained my composure and played it cool. Every few minutes, I would ask the boys what they thought. They'd usually give me a canned, generic answer, but I could tell they were paying attention.

The subsequent videos I allowed them to watch on their own. We have our older boys walk on a treadmill every day if they haven't had any other form of exercise. The treadmill allows them to watch videos or even talk to friends on the phone while getting some movement. They walked while watching the "Do Hard Things" content, and as their hearts were pumping faster with the exercise, their minds were also soaking in the knowledge.

Of all the stories and principles shared in the videos, one stood out to them both. The twins explained how elephants are tamed and trained for work in India. A full-grown elephant has the power to knock over a tall tree with his brute strength, but the elephant will not resist when tied up with a simple rope. The animal will give up at the first sign of resistance.

The reason why the elephant won't break free from a rope is because when the elephant was a baby, the trainer would bind his leg with thick chains and uncomfortable shackles. The baby elephant would fight and strain until the shackles cut into his ankles and caused great pain. Eventually, he would stop fighting against the chain. As time passed and the elephant gave up the fight, the chain would be replaced with a light rope, but he still never fought back.

Even as the elephant grew into adulthood and had the strength to lift heavy logs with his trunk or drag tons of weight with his enormous strength, he still felt powerless against the rope. In his simple mind, he believed he must give up at the first sign of resistance, because in the past he had failed to break free. The elephant had no concept of the strength he possessed, and so he could be easily controlled by something far weaker than himself. He remained in lifelong bondage simply because he didn't know his own strength.

I love the metaphor of these elephants, because it has application to so many areas of life. Your sons are growing up in a world that teaches them to give up at the first sign of resistance. Your sons have vivid memories of times they've tried to break free from something and haven't been able to change their situation. Your sons, like you and me, are tempted to give up as soon as life gets hard.

As it relates to the topic of lust and masturbation, your son may have given up and resigned himself to the myth that he is powerless over his situation. I was in that same place. I was allowing the "rope" of masturbation to keep me bound in a slave-like cycle of lust and self-gratification. I had failed in the past to break free through my own willpower, so in shame and defeat, I believed that I would always be in bondage.

Maybe you feel inadequate to help your son work through the issues he's facing, or maybe even having the conversation terrifies you, but you are stronger than you think you are. You can do difficult things.

Maybe your son feels powerless to break free from the bondage of lust and masturbation, but he is stronger than he thinks. Not only can he do difficult things, he has a power at his disposal that is even greater than the mighty strength of the elephant. You have this same power available to you too.

We have more strength than we realize, but our strength alone will never be enough. Thankfully, our strength alone never has to be enough. Jesus himself wants to fight this battle with us and for us. He's waiting for the invitation.

Praying for strength in areas like masturbation might seem awkward, but no conversation with God should ever feel awkward. Our heavenly Father already sees our struggles and shortcomings. He's never shocked or surprised by our sins. He wants to bring forgiveness and the opportunity for a fresh start.

Have the courage to talk bluntly with your son about these issues. Don't shame him or embarrass him. Listen to him, and allow him to share his struggles. If he won't open up, press him on the issue. If he still won't open up, then share your heart and your guidance.

If you don't know what to say, you might start by talking about the fact that whatever we feed gets bigger. When we overfeed our bodies, our bodies grow bigger. When we feed our bank account with financial deposits, our balance grows bigger. When we feed our lustful thoughts with a steady diet of lust and self-gratification, our desires will grow bigger and eventually give birth to unhealthy expressions of desire.

Challenge your son to carefully consider what he's feeding. Is he feeding his mind and soul with the truth of God's Word? The more Scripture we put into our minds, the more we'll be safeguarding our eyes and hearts from wandering offtrack. The Bible says, "I have hidden your word in my heart, that I might not sin against you" (Ps. 119:11).

If we're not feeding our minds a steady diet of God's living Word, we won't have any appetite for it. If we're feeding our minds a diet of lustful thoughts playing on-demand, our appetites will be driven by lust. Your son will still have a strong sex drive even if he's doing all the right things and fighting hard to protect his thoughts, but if he's feeding his mind the right things, the fight for purity is one he can win. He doesn't have to be bound by the rope of lust when he has the strength to break free.

If your son is believing the lie that he must masturbate to maintain his body, he needs to be reminded that there's no acceptable justification for sin. Lust is a sin, and there's almost certainly lust happening in the mind during masturbation. If the body needs to release semen, God has created a built-in release valve of sorts. It's called a nocturnal emission, or "wet dream." God never puts us in a position where our only choice is to sin. We always have a choice to show restraint.

While your son needs to know the truth about sexual sin, he should also never be made to feel perverted or dirty or weird for having strong desires for sex. Your son should never feel shamed for being attracted to young women or for feeling strong desires for them. That's a healthy desire from God, but expressed at the wrong time or in the wrong way, those desires can sabotage true intimacy and turn respect for women into objectification of women.

As I write these words, I'm again sitting in my three-year-old son Chatham's room watching him slowly fall asleep. After the long, arduous process of getting him to this

> WHILE YOUR SON NEEDS TO KNOW THE TRUTH ABOUT SEXUAL SIN, HE SHOULD ALSO NEVER BE MADE TO FEEL PERVERTED OR DIRTY OR WEIRD FOR HAVING STRONG DESIRES FOR SEX.

point with multiple potty breaks, messy tooth-brushing, bed-time stories, prayer, a last-minute cup of water, and a thousand other distractions to postpone bedtime, he's finally lying down peacefully. Watching him drift off to sleep is the most peaceful part of my day.

As with my older boys, I know Chatham will grow up in a world full of sexually charged imagery, ubiquitous tempta-tion, and broken mind-sets related to sexuality. Right now, he's so innocent and untainted by the lust he'll encounter one day. Part of me wants to shelter him in this bedroom filled with lullabies and stuffed animals and somehow preserve his innocence by never allowing him to encounter temptation, but I know that's not practical.

Instead, I want to have the kind of relationship with him and all my precious sons so that they know they can talk to me about anything. I want them to know that I'm here for them, and I'll love them unconditionally no matter how much they mess up. I also want them to know I love them too much to enable them to sin. I want to provide accountability. I want to provide answers. I want to provide whatever they need, but I also know I'll fall short sometimes.

Above all that I want for them, I want them to know there's a perfect Father who loves them even more than I do, and he will be there for them in ways that I can't. I want my boys to love and follow Jesus. He's the one who faced all temptation and was still without sin. He's the one who looked at women with full respect and never with lust or condemnation in his eyes. He's the one who can forgive and restore when our own actions have caused broken promises and broken hearts.

In Women's Own Words

"I want to marry a guy who looks at me the way my dad looks at my mom. He looks at her like she's the most beautiful woman in the world. There's something so pure and powerful about it. So many boys look at girls like disposable objects for their own pleasure. I won't settle for that. No woman should settle for that."

—MORGAN E. (AGE 16)

"My husband finally quit porn, but his masturbation habit continues. Even though he's not actively watching porn, all those images in his mind are on-demand 24-7 and he'll pleasure himself whenever he feels like it. Whenever I'm in the mood and want to initiate sex, he won't be in the mood because he's already masturbated. It makes me feel ugly and rejected. It feels like a form of infidelity. It's really hurting our marriage, but he doesn't think it's a big deal because he's been doing it since he was in middle school."

—SUSIE B. (AGE 45)

CHAPTER 8

THE MODEL OF MARRIAGE

If a man loves a woman's soul, he will end up loving only one woman, but if he only loves a woman's body or face, then all the women in the world won't satisfy him.

—UNKNOWN

I f you were familiar with any of my work prior to this book, you most likely connected with me through my writing and speaking about marriage. Ashley and I have a passion for helping build stronger marriages, because we believe that stronger marriages create stronger families and stronger families create a better world for future generations. We're also convinced that the way we approach marriage has a massive impact on how our children learn to respect themselves and others.

Most of this book is focused on the lessons that we as parents need to be teaching to our kids, but this chapter will identify the relationship principles we need to model for our children. A marriage-focused chapter in the middle of a book about raising boys might seem out of place, but I'd argue that it might be one of the most important chapters in this book. For those of you who are married, your marriage is the most important example of love and respect between a man and a woman that your kids will ever see. By your daily example, you're showing your sons how they should treat women and you're showing your daughters what they should expect from men.

For those of you who are unmarried, first, I tip my hat to you as one who is tackling the most difficult job on the planet. Your work as a single parent is arduous, but your investment in your son's life is undoubtedly having a profound impact. In addition to all the work you're doing and the weight you're carrying, you're also making time to read this book simply to be a better parent and to raise a more respectful son. I may not know you personally, but please know that I have the utmost respect for you.

I want to discuss the principles and practices that will bring more peace to your home and to all your relationships. The stories and lessons I'll be sharing here will primarily be within the context of the marital relationship, but these same principles will help you thrive in other relationships, including your relationship with your children. It all begins with creating an atmosphere of peace in the home.

THE F5 MARRIAGE TORNADO

Have you ever felt like your marriage was stuck in a cycle of negativity? Without meaning to, you and your spouse keep falling back into the same rut of negativity and criticism, and you're not sure how to get out of it. I think most, if not all, marriages have experienced this at one time or another. This cycle of negativity can create feelings of desperation and hopelessness, and it can also threaten to model the wrong relational examples for our children. Respect is often the first casualty when a negative tone permeates the home.

Most marriages experience seasons with storms of frustration or conflict, but when those seasons turn into the status quo, the marriage's survival is at risk. There are so many factors that lead to this negative cycle. It can be set into motion by stress or exhaustion or miscommunication or a myriad of other things. How it starts isn't nearly as important as how to break out of it, because if you allow the negative cycle to continue, it can devastate your marriage and teach your kids unhealthy lessons that could sabotage their future dating relationships and marriages.

I like to refer to this negative cycle as the F5 Marriage Tornado. My knowledge about tornadoes is limited to what I learned from the classic 1990s movie *Twister*. (Is it just me or were movies way better in the nineties?) I remember that movie teaching that an F5 tornado is the most powerful storm on earth. When you're in the center of an F5 Marriage Tornado, it can definitely feel like the most powerful storm in your life.

Here's how it works: There are five factors in this storm of marital conflict, and they all start with the letter *F* (hence the F5 reference). Each of these factors leads in a cycle to the next one on the list, and with each rotation around all five, the storm grows in ferocity. Maybe you're a visual learner like me, so take a look at this simple graphic explaining the F5 Marriage Tornado, and then I'll unpack how this works:

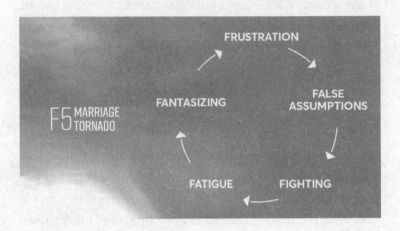

The storm always starts with frustration. We're all prone to frustrations at times. These frustrations might not have anything to do with your spouse, but how you deal with the frustration can have a tremendous impact on how you communicate to your spouse. When you're caught in this storm, frustration always leads to false assumptions.

False assumptions occur when you believe lies that your spouse is against you or that your spouse doesn't care as much as you do about the issue. Once these false assumptions fester, they inevitably lead to fighting, which can become a war of words or a war of nonverbal shots aimed at wounding each other.

The fighting eventually leads to fatigue, and this is

dangerous because we tend to make our worst decisions when we're tired. Fatigue blurs our vision and keeps us from seeing the situation clearly. Fatigue also makes us susceptible to the fifth step in this cyclone, which is fantasizing. When we grow weary from the whole cycle, we can slip into the toxic trap of fantasy in the form of escaping into pornography or romance novels or looking up old flames on social media or just imagining a better life without our spouses.

This process will lead you right back to the start of the storm, but with more frustration, and the cycle continues to repeat itself until one or both spouses either gives up on the marriage or decides to fight for peace.

If you find yourself in this storm that has been the end of far too many marriages, please don't give up. Please don't believe the myth that your marriage will always be caught in this exhausting cycle of negativity and conflict. You have the power to bring peace. The F5 storm has an F5 solution. Here's how it works:

F5 MARRIAGE PEACE PLAN

RAISING BOYS WHO RESPECT GIRLS

The F5 Peace Plan starts with frustration. As I said before, frustration is an inevitable part of life and marriage, but you don't have to let that frustration lead you into the storm cycle. In the peace plan, the moment you feel frustration, you break the negative cycle by choosing forgiveness. Choose to let go of whatever grudge or animosity you're carrying. We don't know who said it first, but it's true that "holding a grudge is like drinking poison and then hoping the other person dies."

Grudges and keeping score of faults will poison your marriage. Choose to forgive, and move forward with grace. This is the first and most important step in finding true and lasting peace in your marriage—and life in general.

After you forgive, follow the apostle Paul's sage advice and fix your thoughts on the good (Phil. 4:8). Don't let your mind fixate on the negative. Whatever captures your focus will seem bigger, so make sure you're focusing on good things. If you're looking for your spouse's flaws, that's all you'll see, but if you're looking for the good, you'll start to see it.

Fixing your thoughts on the positive should be a constant reminder to progress to the next step, which is to focus on God's promises. Remember that God is with you and he is bigger than whatever struggle you're facing. His promises are true and can be trusted. Immerse yourself in God's Word, and choose to trust that God is in control even when life is difficult.

As you do these things, you'll discover a mental and spiritual renewal that leads to the final step, which is finding peace. Real peace is found in the Prince of Peace. When Christ is the center of your thoughts, he will always bring more peace to your perspective. He wants to bring more peace to your heart, your home, and your marriage.

I love this simple peace plan for many reasons, but one of the most practical reasons is that you don't need your spouse to participate with you to do it. You don't have to get stuck in the cynical cycle of excuses that say, "Well, if my husband [wife] would just do their part, then the marriage would be great."

It's never your job to fix or change your spouse. It's your job to love and respect your spouse and to trust God to do the rest.

If you follow this peace plan, even if your spouse isn't currently joining you in the peace process, you'll find that God will start bringing more peace to your home. Your example will eventually be a factor in bringing a change of heart to your spouse too.

Choose to be the first one to stop the fighting. Refuse to keep living in the eye of an F5 Marriage Tornado when peace is within your grasp. Trust the Prince of Peace to calm the storms, and he will. This plan can radically improve your marriage, but it will help your other relationships too. By bringing more peace to your home, you'll also be setting a healthy example for your kids, and you'll have more energy and inspiration to be the kind

> IT'S NEVER YOUR JOB TO FIX OR CHANGE YOUR SPOUSE. IT'S YOUR JOB TO LOVE AND RESPECT YOUR SPOUSE AND TO TRUST GOD TO DO THE REST.

of parent you want to be. Peace is the soil where respect can take root. When you choose peace in your home, respect can flourish for everyone under your roof, starting with your spouse.

WHEN YOUR SPOUSE DOESN'T SHARE YOUR FAITH

As you've already discovered, this book is written from a Christian worldview and perspective. I'm a very imperfect Christian, but my faith guides my life and it is the lens through which I see the world around me and my own place within it. My wife inspires me with her faith and love for Jesus. Our shared faith is the foundation of our marriage, and it keeps us pointed in the same direction with our parenting decisions and all other aspects of our life.

I know that not all couples have the benefit of a shared faith. When one spouse is a Christian and one spouse is not, or when both spouses are in very different places in their own faith journeys, it can cause tension. Different faiths or worldviews can complicate the parenting lessons I've outlined in this book and create confusion and stress within the home. If you're in a storm like the F5 Marriage Tornado I just described, or if you and your spouse have very different parenting perspectives because of different faiths or worldviews, I want to give you some practical guidance.

I recently had the opportunity to meet one of my favorite authors, Lee Strobel. He's written dozens of books about the Christian faith, including the bestseller *The Case for Christ*, which was recently made into a movie. The book tells the extraordinary story of Lee's life and his marriage. Lee was an atheist and a successful journalist when his wife, Leslie, found a church and became a Christian. Lee thought she had lost her mind, so he used his journalism skills to research the Christian faith and attempt to disprove it. Not exactly an act motivated by respect for her. But what happened instead was that the facts he found convinced him that Jesus is real and the Bible is true.

Lee and Leslie struggled in their marriage during those turbulent years when Leslie was wholeheartedly following Christ and Lee was doing everything he could to undermine her faith. Ultimately, Leslie's powerful testimony of love and grace, combined with the evidence of Christianity, led Lee to give his heart to Christ and devote the rest of his life to ministry. Decades later, Lee and Leslie have a wonderful marriage and a solid partnership in their faith and their ministry.

So many couples are in the situation Lee and Leslie were once facing. It can cause tremendous stress on a marriage when one spouse has a devout faith in Christ and the other spouse doesn't. In that situation, both spouses are facing life with different compasses. They're operating from two different worldviews, and it makes unity in marriage an elusive struggle. We often get questions from a desperate husband or wife who wants to know how to connect with their unbelieving spouse.

I was talking with a lady at our church on Sunday, and with tears in her eyes she started to tell me about these same struggles in her marriage. With a trembling voice, she said, "My marriage is falling apart. You might not have even known that I'm married, because my husband never comes to church with me. He's not a Christian. It's like we live on two different planets. Our value systems, beliefs, and worldviews are miles apart. My faith is the most important part of my life, but I can't share it with him because when I do, he just accuses me of preaching at him. I feel like we keep drifting further and further apart. I pray about it every day and I do everything in my power to improve our relationship, but nothing seems to work. What should I do?"

I've been working with married couples for a long time, and as a pastor, one of the biggest marital challenges I hear from people within the church is the same challenge this lady is facing. God knew this scenario could create a lot of heartache, so he gives explicit warnings in the Scriptures for a believer not to marry a nonbeliever. No matter how much chemistry and compatibility you might think you have with someone, if one of you is a Christian and one is not, don't get married. God's commands are always for our protection.

If you're already married, you can't build a time machine, so the Bible's instructions on whom to marry or not marry don't apply. The Bible has very specific instructions for this scenario:

> If a fellow believer has a wife who is not a believer and she is willing to continue living with him, he must not leave her. And if a believing woman has a husband who is not a believer and he is willing to continue living with her, she must not leave him. For the believing wife brings holiness to her marriage, and the believing husband

brings holiness to his marriage. Otherwise, your children would not be holy, but now they are holy. (But if the husband or wife who isn't a believer insists on leaving, let them go. In such cases the believing husband or wife is no longer bound to the other, for God has called you to live in peace.) Don't you wives realize that your husbands might be saved because of you? And don't you husbands realize that your wives might be saved because of you? (1 Cor. 7:12–16 NLT)

In light of this passage and all the Bible has to teach on marriage, I believe every Christian who is married to a nonbeliever should do the following four things to model respect and life-changing love not only to their kids but to their nonbelieving spouses as well:

1. Promote peace.

The passage above reminds us that we are called to live in peace (1 Cor. 7:15). Practically speaking, this means you shouldn't go picking fights with your spouse. Don't try to use guilt, manipulation, or demands to get them to see things from your perspective. Jesus said, "Blessed are the peacemakers" (Matt. 5:9 NIV). Strive to be the one who resolves conflict in your marriage, not the one who starts it.

2. Share your faith by your actions.

Lee Strobel said that his wife Leslie's life became some of the most compelling evidence for Christianity. The most powerful "sermons" come through actions and not just words. You are probably not going to talk your husband or wife into becoming a Christian, but the love and respect you show through your actions can make your faith seem so attractive that he or she might become interested. Even if they never accept Christ, your home is still going to have more peace and joy if you're living out a Christian example of love and grace.

3. Don't try to fix, change, or judge your spouse. Just love your spouse. The rest is God's business.

As a Christian, you're called to love above all else. Remember that love is patient and kind (1 Cor. 13:4), so be patient and kind toward your spouse. You will never be held accountable for the decisions your spouse ultimately makes, but you will be held accountable for how you loved him or her. Don't try to change your spouse; just love your spouse. Love is the primary tool God uses to change us all.

4. Pray and remember that God loves you, and he loves your spouse too.

Prayer is powerful, and it always brings results. Sometimes God uses prayer to change our circumstances, and sometimes he uses prayer to simply change our perspective about our circumstances. Pray for your spouse daily. Pray for his or her salvation. Pray that God would help you to love him or her selflessly. Pray that God would give you strength, grace, and encouragement on those days you feel alone in your marriage. Remember that Jesus is with you, and he's never going to leave you or forsake you.

AVOIDING "THE ROOMMATE TRAP"

One of the worst examples we can teach our kids is to simply give up and start living as roommates instead of living as partners, lovers, best friends, and fully devoted spouses. When our kids grow up only seeing Mom and Dad as roommates or business partners or coparents, we've robbed them of the gift of seeing the kind of marriage that makes them excited to be married someday. I'm convinced one of the biggest reasons for young adults' indifference toward marriage is the fact they grew up in homes where there weren't healthy marriages modeled. They look at their own parents and think, *If that's what marriage is, then it's not for me.*

It's easy to fall into this. No couple walks down the aisle and exchanges vows thinking they'll end up in a lifeless, loveless marriage someday. Still, it happens all the time when a marriage gets on autopilot. Ashley and I receive emails and Facebook messages every day from couples who feel stuck in this situation and are not sure how to break out of it. We recently received a message on Facebook from a wife who was feeling frustrated, discouraged, and hopeless in her marriage. To paraphrase her message, she said,

> I don't know what to do anymore. My husband and I used to be best friends. We used to be in love. I don't know what changed or when it changed, but now it feels like we're just roommates. We're just two strangers sharing a house and sharing bills and sharing kids, but this isn't what I wanted our marriage to be. I'm not sure how to get back to what we had before. I can't keep going on like this. What do I do? Help!

Her struggle is one that probably keeps her awake at night and makes her days much more difficult than they need to be. Her struggle is tragic, but it's not unique. In our work with married couples from all over the world, we've seen a startling trend of many marriages facing similar struggles. Marriages are falling into what I call "the Roommate Trap."

The Roommate Trap isn't like a mousetrap that snaps you in an instant. It's slow and methodical like an elaborate maze. Once a couple enters the maze of life's busyness—work, kids, bills, and so forth—they can find themselves wandering around and getting separated from each other. It's not an intentional separation; it's just what can happen when life is happening fast.

In the maze, a couple gets into a sort of autopilot. Again, it doesn't happen all at once, and it's rarely an intentional choice to pull away from each other. It's subtle.

After a long season of just trying to keep their heads above water, one or both spouses begin to notice that the marriage isn't what it used to be. They're no longer best friends and lovers. There's no longer laughter filling the home. There's no longer much physical affection. They act like roommates and nothing more.

Whether you are one of the countless spouses suffering in silence with this same kind of stagnated marriage or if you're simply wanting to be proactive to keep your marriage from slipping into the Roommate Trap, here are four keys to improving your marriage. When done consistently, these four simple action steps can help get your marriage out of the Roommate Trap and stay strong!

1. Search for solutions instead of assigning blame.

When you're struggling in your marriage or feeling alone and isolated, it's easy to want to assign blame to the other spouse. It's also easy to blame yourself. Neither of those options is helpful. Instead of blaming, show your spouse respect by communicating about what you're feeling. Ask your spouse how he or she is feeling. Start to create some action-oriented steps to bring improvement.

2. Do what you did at the beginning of the relationship.

When couples tell me, "Things were so much better back when we were dating," I usually smile and ask, "Well, then why did you stop dating?" I'm trying to make the point that the dating, romance, and pursuit that happens early in a relationship shouldn't stop just because a couple marries. Sure, there are practical challenges when kids and bills come along, but there are also beautiful blessings in every season of marriage. You shouldn't try to re-create the early days of your marriage, because the current days can be even better, but you can start doing some of the positive things you did at the beginning of the relationship like staying up late just to talk, sending love notes, flirting with each other, and a million other ways to stay connected.

3. Pray with your spouse, and pray for your spouse.

I'm convinced that prayer is one of the most intimate acts a married couple can share. When you pray for your spouse, it changes your perspective about your spouse. It binds you closer together. When you pray with your spouse, it simultaneously

RAISING BOYS WHO RESPECT GIRLS

brings you closer to God and closer to each other. No marriage problem is bigger than God, and when you invite the peace of Christ and the wisdom of the Holy Spirit into your marriage, transformation happens. When you don't know which way to turn, turn to Jesus, and you'll be headed in the right direction.

4. Don't give up!

We live in a culture that teaches us to quit the moment something becomes difficult or uncomfortable. Many people seem more committed to their diets, their hobbies, or their exercise routines than they are committed to their marriages. When your marriage is in a tough spot, refuse to give up. You will get through this, and overcoming the struggle will make your marriage even stronger.

> YOUR KIDS ARE NOTICING HOW YOU AND YOUR SPOUSE TREAT EACH OTHER, AND IT'S THE MOST PROFOUND LESSON ON RELATIONSHIPS YOU COULD EVER TEACH THEM.

The main theme running through all the stories and principles in this chapter is simply to keep fighting for your marriage. Fight for each other and not against each other. Keep pursuing each other. Keep loving and respecting each other.

Your kids are noticing how you and your spouse treat each other, and it's the most profound lesson on relationships you could ever teach them. Be intentional, and make sure you're teaching them a healthy example. Not one of us is perfect, but all of us can be healthy. If you'd like more resources to help you and your spouse continue to build a healthy marriage and a legacy of love and respect in your home, please check out our site at www.DaveAndAshleyWillis.com.

In Women's Own Words

"My husband is so good to me. I always feel respected by him because he listens to me whenever I'm talking. Even if I get emotional about something, he never discounts my feelings or belittles me. He's tender with me, but never in a patronizing or belittling way. He always treats me like his partner and his best friend. I love him so much, and I want our boys to grow up and treat their wives the way their daddy treats me."

—LACRECIA G. (AGE 34)

"Chivalry has never gone out of style. When my husband holds the door open for me or hands me his umbrella on a rainy day, my heart still skips a beat."

—EDNA V. (AGE 76)

"I feel respected by my husband when he runs things by me out of courtesy instead of just making decisions on his own, no matter how small or big. Because we are a team. I like when I'm treated with equality by males even though I'm a female."

—DANIELLE H. (AGE 26)

CHAPTER 9

TEACHING YOUR SON
THE RIGHT LESSONS

I was sitting in church yesterday listening to our pastor preach a powerful message on the adventure of faith God has in store for every believer. I have a self-diagnosed case of adult ADHD, so sometimes my thoughts and my eyes wander around the sanctuary during even the most compelling sermons. On this particular Sunday, my eyes landed on a sight I couldn't believe I was seeing. It was shocking.

Sitting two rows in front of me was an adolescent boy who appeared to be around fourteen years old. He was holding up his smartphone at an angle where I could see it clearly. There was no one sitting in the row directly in front of me, so at the unique angle of my line of sight, I may have been the only other person in the auditorium who could see his screen.

At first glance, I just saw cartoon images. They were female characters from a cartoon my kids watch often. I rolled my eyes in frustration at the ubiquitous plight of kids on screens at inappropriate times. As I looked again to his screen, my frustration turned to horror. His web searches, which at first glance had seemed harmlessly sophomoric, were actually pornographic.

This boy, seated right next to his parents, was brazenly searching the web for cartoon porn. I honestly didn't even know this was a real thing. Some additional research into this topic later revealed some unbelievable global trends. With the worldwide screen addiction epidemic, many men and adolescents are becoming addicted to animated porn created from popular female cartoon and video game characters. In Japan, this problem has become so widespread that there's a national shortage of men willing to marry real women.[1]

This boy at church was cavalierly treading down a dark and dead-end path. Without trying to gawk or cause a scene, I leaned in slightly, trying to make out the images I was seeing. There was no mistake. These female characters from a popular cartoon series had been turned into animated porn stars. His parents had apparently conditioned themselves to giving him "privacy" on his devices, which is both naïve and tragic.

I was sitting too far away to intervene without making a disruptive scene in the middle of church. I sat feeling helpless while a bombardment of thoughts and emotions swirled in my mind. I was frustrated by the pervasiveness of porn at our kids' fingertips. I was terrified by the damaging messages our kids are seeing and hearing every day. I was saddened by the way our kids' minds are being reprogrammed and how this is leading to an epidemic of disrespect toward women—and culminating in so many of the tragic revelations we've been seeing about abuse and harassment. I was more motivated than ever to have important conversations with my own sons about all these things and help other parents do the same.

I've learned so much through the journey of researching and writing this book, and hopefully you've learned some valuable truths as you've read it. While I hope you and I continue learning, what matters most is our effectiveness in teaching these lessons to our sons. If we have heads full of new knowledge but our sons are still drifting in the wrong direction, then our knowledge is useless.

To make sure the principles we've been discussing take root in our sons' hearts and minds, I'm dedicating this final chapter to creating teachable moments with your son around the themes within this book. It will take intentionality on your part and mine, but if we'll create teachable moments with our sons, we can help propel them toward new heights and also strengthen our own family relationships through every unique season of their lives.

It can be difficult to get a boy to open up about what he's thinking and feeling. You've probably already figured that out, and you've probably also learned there's no one-size-fits-all approach to communication, because every person is different. Still, there are some common preferences and perspectives possessed by most males, so knowing this could give you a head start.

Throughout this book I've shared stories, statistics, and

scriptures to prompt healthy conversations, but I want to leave you with one additional practical tool to help drive these principles home in a lasting way. Below is an age-specific guide to starting ongoing conversations with your son around the areas of sex, technology, authentic manhood, and respect for women. The convergence of these four areas will create an intersection where much of his thought life is focused during adolescence.

Knowing how to speak his language can make a big impact. So before I dive into the age-specific breakdown, let me give you one big tip that is valid for males of all ages: most boys are more receptive to communication when it's built around activity. For females, talking itself can be all the activity that's necessary, but most boys don't want to talk just for the sake of talking. Talking is something that happens naturally as a side effect of an activity like walking together, riding bikes together, playing golf together, playing video games together, or a million other activities.

> MOST BOYS ARE MORE RECEPTIVE TO COMMUNICATION WHEN IT'S BUILT AROUND ACTIVITY.

When you tell your son, "We need to talk," chances are good he's going to glaze over or shut down completely. When you ask him to do his favorite activity with you and then let a conversation start happening in the midst of the activity, he'll most likely open up in new ways. This is the single best communication tip I can give to parents of boys: build your conversations around activities.

The questions and activities listed below are designed to

spark ongoing conversation and connection with your son through all the stages of his development into manhood. They're also designed to foster an early and ongoing respect for women. These lists clearly aren't comprehensive, but they'll hopefully start the conversations and cultivate some unique ideas that are perfectly suited for you and your son.

Here's a simple breakdown of how to guide the conversations with your son when he's in preschool, elementary school, high school, and college.

PRESCHOOL

My three-year-old son, Chatham, saw me wearing a fake beard when we went trick-or-treating this year. He pointed at my face and said, "Daddy, you're dressed up like a man!" I laughed and then thought to myself, *Wait! If he thinks I'm dressed up like a man now, what the heck does he think I actually am when I'm not wearing a fake beard?* It became a funny teaching moment when I got to explain that being a man is about much more than having a beard.

Preschool is an age of exploration when your son is discovering the world around him and his unique place within it. It's the perfect time to start conversations about the God-given uniqueness of boys and girls and to celebrate those God-given differences. It's also a time to start fostering healthy relationships with other boys and with girls. Let your son learn from a young age to have healthy and respectful interactions with males and females of all ages.

Questions to prompt conversations with your son:

1. What's one thing you love about Mommy?
2. Who is your favorite girl superhero?
3. What's your favorite thing about your preschool teacher (or another positive female role model)?

Activities to prompt conversations with your son:

1. Intentionally set up play dates with girls his age. Obviously, let your son play with other boys, too, but make it natural from an early age for your son to interact with girls as friends, peers, and equals.
2. Read bedtime stories and Bible stories that focus on the strength and courage of both male and female characters.
3. Watch cartoons and movies that display healthy interactions between males and females.

ELEMENTARY SCHOOL

My son Chandler is currently in the first grade. He's masculine, athletic, and "all boy" in every sense, but he's also drawn to friends of both genders. How he plays with his friends often looks different based on the individual personalities and gender percentages in the group, but he enjoys playing with girls as much as he enjoys playing with boys. He seems to be on a track toward healthy future friendships with both genders. He also doesn't tend to make generalizations many boys his age make by saying things like "You throw like a girl" or other negative or limiting connotations about females. These questions and activities have helped give him a head start, and they could help your elementary-aged sons as well.

Questions to prompt conversations with your son:

1. What's one thing that makes Mommy so strong?
2. Who is your favorite girl character in the Bible?
3. When you grow up and become a daddy, what kinds of things will you want to do with your wife and your kids?

Activities to prompt conversations with your son:

1. Encourage your son to play at least one sport in a coed league. Learning to see both boys and girls as equal teammates is great training for learning respect.
2. Encourage forms of entertainment, games, and video games that involve protecting women (for instance, saving the princess) and also showcase stories of strong women doing the rescuing. These various examples will help him aspire to be both a protector and a respecter of women.
3. Read bedtime stories and Bible stories that reinforce lessons of courage and chivalry.

MIDDLE SCHOOL

We have two sons currently in middle school. Cooper and Connor are extraordinary young men who embody valiant masculinity while also being sensitive, respectful, and conscientious toward their female peers and women of all ages. We're giving extra attention to our conversations with Cooper and Connor related to puberty, sex, porn, and the other themes addressed in this book because they're at critical ages where their thoughts and actions are forming into potentially lifelong behaviors. We're proud of the paths they're choosing. These questions and activities are some of what we're using to coach and encourage them on their journeys.

Questions to prompt conversations with your son:

1. Of all the women in history (besides me/Mom), what woman do you respect the most? What do you believe were her greatest strengths?
2. I've heard that some middle school kids are sexting (sending sexually explicit pictures to each other from their smartphones). Do you think this is happening at your school? (I'm sure it is happening at their school, but leaving the question open-ended might spark some conversation.)
3. What's one thing you think boys don't understand about girls?

4. What's one thing you think girls don't understand about boys?

Activities to prompt conversations with your son:

1. Start watching the news together in the morning before school or in the evening before bedtime. Strategically talk to him about stories featuring a female hero or stories featuring a female who has been victimized by a man. Never demonize men or make it a male-versus-female false dichotomy, but challenge him to be a respecter and protector of women so the women and girls in his life never have to be victimized.

2. Have healthy and transparent ongoing conversations about sex. The resources Passport2Purity and Passport2Identity from FamilyLife Today are wonderful tools to help facilitate these ongoing conversations with your middle school son.[2]

3. Closely monitor his online activity. Filtering software such as X3Watch or Covenant Eyes can help you block porn while also monitoring which sites he's visiting. His online activity will give you a unique insight into his thought process and create a starting point for engaging conversations.

4. Listen when your son wants to talk. We've found that important conversations can be initiated by our boys at unlikely times and around unlikely subjects, but when we are willing to put our phones down and intently

listen to whatever they want to discuss, it often leads to memorable and meaningful conversations.

HIGH SCHOOL

Ashley and I both have a lot of experience with high school students, but it hasn't (yet) come from parenting. Ashley has been a middle school and high school teacher, and we've both spent years working together in youth ministry. In fact, we were working with high school students as church leaders even before we had children of our own. The lessons we've learned from these experiences have shaped the types of questions and activities we hope to share with our sons when they're in high school.

Questions to prompt conversations with your son:

1. I read that statistically there are fewer high school students having sex than there were in my generation. I'm proud of you guys! Why do you think more kids are choosing to wait to have sex?

2. What are the traits you believe make a good wife? What are the traits that make a good husband? Who is one married couple (other than those in our family) who has the kind of marriage you'd like to have someday?

3. What do you believe are the toughest challenges young men in your school are facing? What would help most?

4. What do you believe are the toughest challenges young ladies in your school are facing? How might you be able to help them?

Activities to prompt conversations with your son:

1. Take your son to a movie with a strong female lead, and then go to his favorite restaurant afterward and talk about the movie and what traits made that female character so strong.

2. Plan one-on-one time with your son. Both parents should regularly spend individual time with each son built around activities your son enjoys. At least once a year during high school, plan a one-on-one overnight trip to reconnect and have deeper conversations.

3. Plan rite-of-passage events around key milestones. I share extensively on these types of events in the chapter on authentic manhood. Make these special events a regular fixture in your family's calendar, when you can publicly honor and celebrate your son's manhood and the traits of integrity and honor he's embodying.

4. Encourage your son to volunteer in a place where he can use his unique gifts to help the community. Make sure the volunteer opportunity has at least one element of helping women. Incentivize his volunteering and celebrate it. Talk to him about his experience.

COLLEGE

The college years are a critical time in a man's life. As I've addressed throughout this book, university campuses have been ground zero for some of the worst crimes being committed against women. They have also been the birthplace of encouraging progress in men taking responsibility to embody honor and respect toward women. In my time teaching on college campuses, I saw firsthand that there are countless opportunities for wise or reckless choices among students. Those choices can have a lifelong impact either positively or negatively.

Questions to prompt conversations with your son:

1. Do you believe women on campus have the same opportunities as men? Does anything seem unfair to one gender?
2. Would you want your future children to have a college experience similar to the one you're having? What would you want your sons to experience? What would you want your daughters to experience?
3. What's something you wish you could tell yourself back in high school that would have prepared you for the challenges you're facing now?
4. What are the traits you would look for in a potential wife? Are there any young ladies on campus you've met who seem to possess those traits?

Activities to prompt conversations with your son:

1. *Ask what books he's required to read this semester.* Choose one of his homework books written by a female author, and tell him you want to buy a copy, read it, and

talk about it with him. Start your own two-member book club.

2. *Volunteer at a charity focused on helping women.* Specifically, choosing a battered women's shelter or a homeless women's shelter could help create meaningful moments and ignite a desire to be a lifelong protector of women. (Please note that the vetting process may be extensive. Background checks and extensive training are likely required.)

3. *Have the courage to share both the wise and poor choices you made in college or young adulthood.* Be willing to talk about your regrets, including past sexual choices. This might be an uncomfortable conversation, but having the courage to be transparent and vulnerable will build trust with your son and also potentially help him learn from both your mistakes and your wise choices.

4. *Look for ways to stay connected.* Don't stalk your son. Let him have wings, but also make sure he knows you're always there for him. Send him encouraging text messages. Send him care packages with goodies from home and with little practical items to make his life easier. You're transitioning your relationship from one of authority and protection over him to one of adult friendship. Let him know you're praying for him daily and you're so proud of the man he has become. Your influence in his life will be life-long if you're willing to navigate these college years

with wisdom by giving him the support he still needs from you.

CREATING TEACHABLE MOMENTS WITH YOUR SONS

There's certainly no shortage of information to teach our sons, but the greater struggle for most parents seems to be finding the right moments to teach it. These teachable moments can be elusive if we're just waiting around for them to happen. We can be tempted to allow the myth of finding the "perfect time" to keep us from having these conversations. We're always going to have to compete with our boys' lack of attention, video game phases, hyperactivity, jokes about poop, and a million other distractions. Don't let those distractions discourage you. Enter into your sons' worlds in every phase of their lives, and meet them where they are.

THE TRUTH IS, THERE'S NO SUCH THING AS PERFECT TIMING. THERE'S ONLY THIS MOMENT AND WHAT YOU CHOOSE TO DO WITH IT.

The truth is, there's no such thing as perfect timing. There's only this moment and what you choose to do with it. There's also no such thing as perfect words or perfect parents. There are no perfect parents and there are no perfect children, but if you'll be a constant presence in your kids' lives, there will be plenty of perfect moments along the way.

It all starts with being present and then looking for those teachable moments. Some of my best conversations with my boys happen when there's the least competition for their attention. I've found bedtime is a powerful nightly opportunity for great interactions because I suddenly become the most interesting guy in the world when my boys are trying to avoid going to sleep. They might ignore me all day, but at bedtime, I have a captive audience. Take advantage of those interruption-free moments in your daily rhythm. They might be rare, but they're always worth grabbing.

I've also had some great opportunities for teachable moments through coaching my kids' sports teams. I've never been a great coach or a great athlete, but I try to be a great encourager. I look for opportunities to encourage my kids and the other kids on the team, and I've learned that encouragement can be one of the most powerful teachers of all.

One winter I was coaching my son Connor's basketball team when he was six years old. It was in a league where boys and girls played together. Our team was made up of six boys and one little girl named Madison. She was taller than most of the boys and was one of the hardest-working players on the team. During one of our scrimmages when I had the kids playing against each other in two teams of three, Madison stole the ball from my son. It was a clean steal and she was on the other team at the time, so she was doing exactly what she was supposed to do.

Connor reacted in a way that surprised and disappointed me. He yelled at her and said, "Why did you take the ball from me? You don't even belong here. Girls shouldn't be allowed to play with boys!"

Madison's lip started quivering. Tears welled up in her eyes, but she quickly wiped them away. She was hurt by Connor's mean-spirited words, and she was embarrassed that she had shown emotion because of the pain. In that moment, I thought about how most little girls and women probably have experiences like this throughout their whole lives. It's wrong.

I immediately called the team together for a quick huddle. Getting six-year-olds to come together in a group and remain quiet for a lesson is like trying to herd a bunch of monkeys who have been drinking Mountain Dew. Still, we managed to get the group together, and I said something like this: "Hey team, I'm really proud of how hard you're working, but on our team, we need to build each other up and never try to hurt each other's feelings. Connor just said something very mean to Madison by telling her that she shouldn't be allowed to play because she's a girl. The truth is that Madison is one of the hardest-working players on this whole team, and we could all learn a lot by watching how she plays. She's also had to show a lot of courage being the only girl on our team, and you boys need to give her the respect she deserves. I'm going to start by implementing a new award. It's called the 'Red Cheeks Award.' It goes to the player who gets the sweatiest or reddest cheeks, because that means they're working extra hard. Cheeks don't lie! Madison wins the prize, because her face is always sweaty, which means she's always working hard. Thank you, Madison, for setting such a great example for us. We're so proud of you and glad you're on our team."

I then had Connor publicly apologize to Madison, and they hugged. The kids immediately went back to playing and started working as hard as they could, all trying to get cheeks as red and sweaty as Madison's. She became the leader they were trying to emulate. All I'd done was shift their definition of winning at basketball from a broken criteria of "you have to be a boy to win" to an inclusive one of "whoever works the hardest and does their personal best is someone to emulate."

Connor grew a lot that year. I don't normally call out one of my sons by name for less-than-flattering behavior, but I told this story about Connor so I could also brag about him. As a young man in sixth grade now, he's so respectful to girls and women. I'm very proud of him.

Last year, Connor's friend Claire had a violin recital. Connor doesn't like recitals but he loves his friend Claire, so he wanted to go. Ashley told him that going meant he would have to dress up in khaki pants and a nice shirt. Connor would rather be naked than wear dress clothes, but once Ashley explained it was a way to show respect to Claire, he meticulously groomed himself. He's never smelled so good in his life! Connor didn't realize it at the time, but Ashley was using this event as a teachable moment.

Connor also wanted to give Claire flowers before her performance. He was so proud to hand them to her and tell her he couldn't wait to hear her play. When Claire began playing, Connor held his breath and hung on her every note. He was intensely focused on her performance and wanted for her to feel good about it. Some other kids started whispering, and Connor, who isn't normally confrontational, called them out and whispered with an authoritative sharpness in his tone, "Hey! Show some respect. Be quiet until she's finished playing."

I'm so proud of the way Connor respects and honors others. He has a heart of gold. He's going to be a great husband and dad someday.

Our other sons are on the right track as well—mostly because of their amazing mother's influence and example. Our oldest son, Cooper, recently went through a program called Social, which teaches preteens and teenagers respect and etiquette. He was placed with a female partner named Megan. Each week Cooper and Megan, along with a hundred other kids, learned dances, dinner etiquette, and how to respectfully interact with the opposite sex. It was a weekly ritual full of teachable moments, plus all the moments afterward when I got to quiz him on everything that happened.

Cooper complained at first, because he thought the whole thing sounded lame, but he ended up loving it. Every Thursday night, he'd put on a blazer and a tie and head off to learn some new dances. After each weekly dance practice, all the kids would walk across the street and hang out at Dairy Queen, which became a highlight of his entire week. When the season ended, the kids had a big dance that resembled a royal gala or something out of *Downton Abbey*. They all looked and felt so grown-up.

Much good happened as a result of Cooper's experience with Social. First, we have some pictures that will be pretty entertaining to him later in life, because he was the shortest boy in Social and Megan was the tallest girl. Being partnered required some courage on both their parts, and their pictures together are adorable.

Much more important than cute pictures, though, is that

I watched Cooper mature through this process. He wasn't just learning stuffy etiquette and dance moves; he was experiencing the fun and freedom that happens when boys and girls learn to interact with each other in respectful ways. I saw his self-confidence increase. I watched his ability to communicate respectfully with the opposite sex improve dramatically. I'm so thankful we made the investment to allow him to be part of Social. I think he's grateful for the experience too.

Chandler is our first-grader, and recently he came home from school telling a story that was one of the sweetest and most thoughtful examples of respect I could imagine. It really warmed my heart. Chandler walked in the door and resolutely declared, "I don't want peanut butter and jelly sandwiches in my lunch anymore."

Ashley and I were surprised by his statement because Chandler loves peanut butter and jelly. He gets that from me. I could eat PB&J multiple times every day, and "Chan Man" and I have that in common. We asked him why he wanted to give up his favorite sandwich, and he said, "My friend Chloe is allergic to peanuts. If she gets around peanut butter she gets sick. She has to sit at a table in the lunchroom where no peanuts are allowed, and I want to sit with her, so I want you to pack me a turkey sandwich from now on so I can sit next to Chloe."

Wow! I was so proud. He's the one who taught me that time! We're all pretty selfish by nature, but my first-grader was learning that a sacrifice made out of love and respect for a friend is always a sacrifice worth making. Honestly, his simple gesture of thoughtfulness challenged me to be less selfish. As parents, we get so preoccupied with all the lessons we think we're supposed to teach our kids that we sometimes forget about all the lessons we can learn from our kids.

With our youngest son, Chatham, we're always looking for ways to start conversations about respect early. He takes after his sweet mama, so he's already one of the kindest toddlers on the planet. We're each a work in progress, but I hope our family continues to set healthy examples for him to follow as he grows. He wants to be a superhero when he grows up. We are trying to help him realize that respect is one of the greatest superpowers of all.

In an all-boy household, there are obviously no sisters around, but through sports, school, and extended family gatherings, we try to be proactive in creating teachable moments. Our little guys are precious, and they want to be just like their big brothers someday. I challenge the older boys to use their influence for good because there are little feet longing to follow in their footsteps.

For all of us, it's important to walk a path worthy of emulation. Especially for those of us who are parents, we must remember that our words, attitudes, and actions are most likely going to be remembered and emulated by our children. Your example is their most influential teacher. None of us are perfect, but all of us can choose the right path. We must. So much is at stake.

MOVING FORWARD WITH NEW PERSPECTIVE

As you process all you've read up to this point, perhaps your head is spinning as you consider what your next steps should be. There are many applications that we as parents need to make based on the information we've learned, but I want to propose a first step that might seem unlikely. It requires a simple shift in perspective. This final story will help illustrate.

In 2012, a talented up-and-coming screenwriter named Jennifer Lee was completing work on a Disney movie called *Wreck-It Ralph* when she was invited to come play a big role on Disney's newest project. The new movie would be called *Frozen*, and it would be unlike anything the studio had ever produced. Tens of millions of dollars had already been invested into the project, but it had hit a roadblock. They were close to pulling the plug altogether.

The movie was facing many setbacks, but one of the most urgent was the storyline. The plot seemed stuck. The characters weren't developing, and the songs weren't coming. Jennifer was brought in to help lead the writing effort and to codirect the film, which also made her Disney's first female feature-film director ever.

Jennifer carefully studied the script and scrutinized the characters. She quickly recognized that the story had unlimited potential, but before they could move forward, the writers needed to reimagine one key character. Up until that point, the main character of Elsa had been a villain. She was the cold and remorseless Snow Queen with no redeemable characteristics. Jennifer brilliantly proposed that the story would only work if Elsa became one of the story's heroes. Like all heroes, she would be complicated and imperfect, but her heart would be good, and, in the end, she would be a vital part of creating a happy ending. Once the character of Elsa was reimagined and rewritten, the rest of the story came together perfectly. The songs began to flow. They were belting out "Let It Go" in no time.

The rest is cinematic history. Jennifer Lee and her team at Disney created one of the most beloved and successful movies in history, spawning a multibillion-dollar franchise, including music, toys, costumes, spinoffs, and a Broadway musical. You're probably humming a *Frozen* song in your head right now.

I share this story because I see some important parallels between the film's progress and our collective progress around the issue of respect and equal opportunities for women and girls. Much progress has been made and much money has been invested, but it feels like we've gotten stuck in a rut before reaching the finish line.

In our frustration, we're quick to diagnose what needs to happen next. Some believe it requires rewriting the laws. Others believe the focus should be on education or on changing the climate in the corporate workplace. While all those proposed focuses have merit, I'm proposing something different. What if, like Jennifer Lee's approach to *Frozen*, we need to begin by simply reimagining one key character in the story?

The key character in this story is you (and me). What if each of us reimagined the roles and responsibilities we have in bringing resolution to this issue for the next generation? What if our change of heart and change of attitude also marked a powerfully effective change of parenting that could help our children right some wrongs that have been left unfinished by previous generations? What if our generation could be the last one to ever experience inequality?

Yes, we need legislation, we need cultural change, we need accountability, we need respect, we need lots of things. But as we're publicly passing judgment on all the prominent figures who have fallen, we should also make an honest self-evaluation about our own thoughts and actions. We have all been part of the problem, and until we have the courage to admit that, we'll never find a lasting solution. Change begins by reexamining our own part in this story and then committing to teach our children to do the same.

Thank you for taking this journey with me. Thank you for believing that our sons and daughters deserve better than their present reality. Thank you for having the courage to put your convictions into action.

Together, we have the power to bring lasting change. I want to create a better world for our sons and our daughters, and I know you want the same. Our desires alone won't bring change, but our actions will. Let's do this!

> CHANGE BEGINS BY REEXAMINING OUR OWN PART IN THIS STORY AND THEN COMMITTING TO TEACH OUR CHILDREN TO DO THE SAME.

In Women's Own Words

"I'm so proud of the young men my sons are growing up to become. They're not perfect, but they have genuine character plus genuine concern for others. I can't take credit for all their positive traits, but I'm so proud to be their mom."

—SHANNON P. (AGE 36)

"I kind of feel sorry for boys today, because they probably feel like they can't do anything right. If they hold the doors open for girls, they're told they're being sexist. If they don't show any chivalry, they're told they're being jerks. I know girls have been given a lot of disrespect and double standards over the years; but honestly, I feel like boys have it harder than girls today. Whatever they do, there's somebody waiting to tell them they're doing it wrong."

—KRISTY D. (AGE 21)

"Of all the things I've done in my life, I'm proudest of the time I spent with my sons. They grew to be such honorable men. I never had a daughter, but I now have wonderful daughters-in-law and I love them like they're my own girls. I've never been rich or famous, but I feel like the richest woman on earth because I raised sons who love their wives and their kids. That's a world-changing legacy."

—MAYA C. (AGE 67)

A LETTER TO MY SONS

My dad sent me a handwritten letter not long ago. It was a simple yet beautiful couple of pages recording his advice, his perspective, and his love for me. It's something I'll treasure forever because it's from him. And I want to do the same for my sons.

As parents, our words have such profound power. We can build our kids up, or we can tear them down. I want my words to be a source of life and hope for my boys. I hope you will read this letter and consider writing one of your own to your children. Above all, I hope my sons will read this someday and be reminded of how much I love them.

Cooper, Connor, Chandler, and Chatham,

You guys are too young to care anything about reading Dad's book right now, but one day I hope you stumble across this and get something out of it. Above everything else I write, always know that you are loved. You are each a gift from God, and your mom and I are so blessed to be your parents!

This book has been primarily about how and why to respect women. I hope these lessons grip your hearts and you grow to be men who will honor, respect, and protect women. I pray you'll choose a path of integrity worthy of your future wife's respect. I pray you'll find a godly wife with the kind of strength, integrity, and faith your mom has. I pray you'll follow God's standards in your choices related to sex and marriage. His ways are perfect, and he has a perfect plan for each of you.

As you grow and begin dating, please always respect yourselves and respect young ladies as well. Never trade temporary pleasure for permanent regret. God's grace is limitless and his forgiveness is available when we sin, but there can still be lasting scars from compromising God's standards for sex and relationships. Protect your own purity, and protect the purity of others as well. Authentic manhood isn't measured by sexual conquests, but rather by sexual restraint. When you choose to live by God's standard for sexual purity, you're showing respect for yourself, for God, and for your future wife.

I've tried to set the right example for you in these areas, but as you well know, your dad is far from perfect! I will continue to try and live out an example worth following, but above all, I pray you'll follow in the footsteps of the only perfect Father. When you're following Jesus, you'll always be headed in the right direction. When he is your guide, you'll never be lost. Make his words and his example the foundation for your choices and the compass to guide your steps.

I love you guys more than you can imagine. Apart from God's grace and your mother's love, being your dad is the greatest gift of my life. I'm eternally grateful for each of you, and I'm so proud of you. I always will be. Remember that there's no mistake you could ever make that is bigger than God's grace. Your mom and I will always be your biggest fans!

Love,
Dad

ACKNOWLEDGMENTS

My name might be the one on the cover, but there are countless names responsible for shaping this book. There are more people to thank than I can possibly list here, but I want to publicly show gratitude and respect to a few who have been instrumental in this journey.

Ashley, your love fuels me. Being your husband, partner, and best friend is the greatest honor of my life. Thank you for all you do for our family. This book, like most things in my life, would not have been possible without you. I love you so much.

Mom and Dad, thank you for raising me in a home full of love, laughter, encouragement, and authentic faith. Your love for each other, your love for Jesus, and your love for us gave me such a solid foundation for life. I still want to be like you guys when I grow up.

The team at Thomas Nelson has once again knocked it out of the park! It's such a privilege to work alongside you. I'm so grateful to the world's best editor, Jessica Wong, for championing the message of this book and making the message more clear, focused, and grammatically correct than it would have ever been had I been writing it without her help and guidance!

Thank you to my literary agent, Amanda Luedeke, whose early enthusiasm for this book is one of the main reasons I had the courage to write it.

Special thanks to my friend and colleague Shaunti Feldhahn, who shared invaluable research with me early in the writing process. Her insights and encouragement ultimately helped shape the direction of the entire book. If you aren't reading her books, you should start!

Thank you to the Evans family and the entire team at MarriageToday and XOmarriage.com. It's such a joy to do life and ministry alongside you. Thank you for your friendship and for the countless ways you've invested in my family.

Thank you to all the women and all the men who challenged my thinking and shaped the content of this book by sharing your own wisdom and life experiences. This book and my life are much richer because of your perspective.

Finally, I want to thank you, the reader, for reading this book. Thank you for investing your time to create a better world for our kids. Thank you for joining me in this journey. Let's keep going. We're headed in the right direction, but there's much work left to be done. Our sons and our daughters are counting on us.

NOTES

Introduction

1. Warren Farrell and John Gray, *The Boy Crisis: Why Our Boys Are Struggling and What We Can Do About It* (Dallas: BenBella Books, 2018), 3.

Chapter 1: The Current Crisis

1. Nic Wirtz and Azam Ahmed, "Before Fatal Fire, Trouble Abounded at Guatemala Children's Home," *New York Times*, March 8, 2017, https://www.un.org/sustainabledevelopment/blog/2016/12/report-majority-of-trafficking-victims-are-women-and-girls-one-third-children/.
2. "Report: Majority of Trafficking Victims Are Women and Girls; One-Third Children," UN News, December 21, 2016, https://news.un.org/en/story/2016/12/548302-majority-trafficking-victims-are-women-and-girls-one-third-children-new-un.
3. "Majority of Trafficking Victims," UN News.
4. "Statistics," National Coalition Against Domestic Violence (NCADV), https://ncadv.org/statistics.
5. Danielle Campoamor, "Ariana Grande Reminds Us Women Have No Safe Place in America," CNN, September 4, 2018,

https://www.cnn.com/2018/09/03/opinions/ariana-grande
-aretha-franklin-funeral-campoamor/index.html.

6. Tyler Kingkade, "Nearly One-Third of College Men in Study
Say They Would Commit Rape," HuffPost, January 9, 2015,
https://www.huffingtonpost.com/2015/01/09/college-men
-commit-rape-study_n_6445510.html.

7. M. J. Lee, Sunlen Serfaty, and Juana Summers, "Congress Paid
Out $17 Million in Settlements. Here's Why We Know So
Little About That Money," CNN, November 16, 2017, https://
www.cnn.com/2017/11/16/politics/settlements-congress
-sexual-harassment/index.html.

8. Michelle Krupa, "The Alarming Rise of Female Genital
Mutilation in America," CNN, updated July 14, 2017, https://
www.cnn.com/2017/05/11/health/female-genital-mutilation
-fgm-explainer-trnd/index.html.

9. "Child Marriage Around the World," International Center for
Research on Women (ICRW), https://www.icrw.org/child
-marriage-facts-and-figures/.

10. "Sexual Assault Statistics," National Sexual Violence Resource
Center (NSVRC), https://www.nsvrc.org/statistics.

11. "Sexual Assault Statistics," NSVRC.

12. "The Most Up-to-Date Pornography Statistics," Covenant
Eyes, www.covenanteyes.com/pornstats.

13. "25 Discrimination Against Women in the Workplace
Statistics," Brandon Gaille, May 29, 2017, https://brandon
gaille.com/23-discrimination-against-women-in-the-workplace
-statistics/.

14. "Media Literacy," Teen Health and the Media, https://depts
.washington.edu/thmedia/view.cgi?section=medialiteracy
&page=fastfacts.

15. Oliver Harvey, Emma Parry, James Beal, and Nick Parker,
"Inside the Horror Sex Slave Cult NXIVM That Blackmailed,

Starved, and Branded Women's Flesh with the Founder's Initials," *Sun*, last updated April 23, 2018, https://www.thesun.co.uk/news/6117325/inside-horror-sex-slave-cult-nxivm/.

16. Tweets posted under #WhyIDidntReport, Twitter, September 21–24, 2018.

17. Ashley Massey (@IAmCardiganGirl), Twitter, September 23, 2018, https://twitter.com/IAmCardiganGirl/status/10439489 36271187968.

18. Zeze (@CherlyStrayed), Twitter, post removed.

19. Barbara Chapnick (@WhyNotBikeThere), Twitter, September 24, 2018, https://twitter.com/whynotbikethere/status/10442 36004826079234.

20. Tertiary Person (@KayThird), Twitter, September 23, 2018, https://twitter.com/kaythird/status/1043953435039555584.

21. PPNYC Action Fund (@PPNYCAction), Twitter, September 24, 2018, https://twitter.com/PPNYCAction/status/1044249 457737519105.

22. *Up and Vanished*, season one, podcast, directed by Payne Lindsey and Donald Albright, https://season1.upandvanished.com/.

Chapter 2: Jesus, Respecter of Women

1. Wayne Grudem, *Evangelical Feminism and Biblical Truth* (Wheaton, IL: Crossway, 2004), 161.

2. Emma Green, "Beth Moore: The Evangelical Superstar Taking on Trump," *Atlantic* (October 2018), https://www.theatlantic.com/magazine/archive/2018/10/beth-moore-bible-study/568288/.

3. John Huffman, "Telemachus: One Man Empties the Roman Coliseum," Discerning History, September 15, 2016, http://discerninghistory.com/2016/09/telemachus-one-man-empties-the-roman-coliseum/.

4. "Telemachus," OrthodoxWiki, October 22, 2012, https://orthodoxwiki.org/Telemachus.

Chapter 3: The Locker Room Mentality

1. George Gilder, *Men and Marriage* (Gretna, LA: Pelican Publishing, 1992), 34.
2. Tim Wright, *Searching for Tom Sawyer* (Bloomington, IN: Westbow Press, 2013), 55.
3. Robert Lewis, *Raising a Modern-Day Knight* (Carol Stream, IL: Tyndale, 1997), 47.
4. "Ballerina Speaks Out on Lawsuit over Alleged Sharing of Nude Photos," ABC News, https://abcnews.go.com/GMA /News/video/ballerina-speaks-lawsuit-alleged-sharing-nude -photos-57667029.

Chapter 4: What Does It Mean to Be a "Real Man"?

1. "Shadow-Boxing Tough Guy Should Protect Home-Alone Japanese Women," Reuters, April 21, 2018, https://www.reuters .com/article/us-japan-shadow-boyfriend/shadow-boxing-tough -guy-should-protect-home-alone-japanese-women-idUSKBN1HS09E.

Chapter 5: The Naked Truth About Sex

1. "Passport2Purity," FamilyLife Today, https://shop.familylife .com/t-fl-passport2purity.aspx.
2. Stephen Arterburn and Fred Stoeker, *Every Young Man's Battle* (Colorado Springs, CO: Waterbrook, 2002), 218.
3. Alan D. DeSantis, *Inside Greek U.: Fraternities, Sororities, and the Pursuit of Pleasure, Power, and Prestige* (Lexington: University Press of Kentucky, 2007), 69.
4. Roland Warren, "Your Past Sins Hindering Your Parent/Child Relationship Today? Read This," Patheos, July 1, 2018, https:// www.patheos.com/blogs/rolandwarren/2018/07/past-sins -hinder-parent-child-relationship/.

Chapter 6: The Porn Epidemic

1. "Pornography Statistics," Covenant Eyes (see ch. 1, n. 12).

2. "Pornography Statistics," Covenant Eyes.

3. "Pornography Statistics," Covenant Eyes.

4. For more information, visit Circle: https://meetcircle.com; Covenant Eyes: https://www.covenanteyes.com; and X3Watch: https://x3watch.com.

5. Mo Isom, *Sex, Jesus, and the Conversations the Church Forgot* (Grand Rapids, MI: Baker, 2018), 64.

6. Josh McDowell Ministry, *The Porn Phenomenon: The Impact of Pornography in the Digital Age* (Ventura, CA: Barna Group, 2016).

7. Judith Reisman, Jeffrey Satinover, Mary Anne Layden, and James B. Weaver, "Hearing on the Brain Science Behind Pornography Addiction and the Effects of Addiction on Families and Communities," Hearing of US Senate Committee on Commerce, Science & Transportation, November 18, 2004, http://www.hudsonbyblow.com/wp-content/uploads/2018/01/2004SenateTestimony.pdf.

8. Steven Stack, Ira Wasserman, and Roger Kern, "Adult Social Bonds and Use of Internet Pornography," *Social Science Quarterly* 85 (March 2004): 75–88.

9. Isom, *Sex, Jesus, and the Conversations*, 22.

10. Jennifer P. Schneider, "Effects of Cybersex Addiction on the Family: Results of a Survey," *Sexual Addiction and Compulsivity: The Journal of Treatment and Prevention* 7, no. 1–2 (2000), 31–58.

11. Samuel L. Perry and Cyrus Schleifer, "Till Porn Do Us Part? A Longitudinal Examination of Pornography Use and Divorce," *Journal of Sex Research* 55, no. 3 (2018), 284–96.

12. Jon K. Uhler, MS, LPC (@JonKUhlerLPC), Twitter, December 4, 2018, https://twitter.com/JonKUhlerLPC/status/107007 1490022825985.

13. Bianca Britton, "Facebook Under Fire for Posts on Auction of Child Bride," CNN, November 23, 2018, https://www.cnn

.com/2018/11/20/africa/south-sudan-child-bride-facebook-auction-intl/index.html.

14. Deborah Wrigley, "Toronto Businessman Brings Sex Robot Brothel to the Galleria Area," ABC 13 News, September 21, 2018, https://abc13.com/technology/toronto-businessman -brings-sex-robot-brothel-to-the-galleria-area-/4306146/.

Chapter 7: Lust and Masturbation

1. Shaunti Feldhahn and Craig Gross, *Through a Man's Eyes: Helping Women Understand the Visual Nature of Men* (Colorado Springs, CO: Multnomah, 2015).
2. Max Lucado, *Anxious for Nothing: Finding Calm in a Chaotic World* (Nashville: Thomas Nelson, 2017), 121.
3. Jeff Feldhahn and Eric Rice, *For Young Men Only: A Guy's Guide to the Alien Gender* (Colorado Springs, CO: Multnomah, 2008), 136.
4. Feldhahn and Gross, *Through a Man's Eyes*, 23.
5. Alex Harris and Brett Harris, "Do Hard Things Conference," DVDs, The Rebelution, https://www.dohardthings.com /conference.

Chapter 9: Teaching Your Son the Right Lessons

1. Tracy McVeigh, "For Japan's 'Stranded Singles,' Virtual Love Beats the Real Thing," *Guardian*, November 19, 2016, https:// www.theguardian.com/world/2016/nov/20/japan-stranded -singles-virtual-love.
2. Passport2Purity (https://shop.familylife.com/t-fl-passport 2purity.aspx) and Passport2Identity (https://shop.familylife .com/t-fl-passport2identity.aspx) are available from FamilyLife Today at https://www.familylife.com/.

D ave Willis spent thirteen years as a full-time pastor and is now a speaker, author, relationship coach, and television host for MarriageToday. He works with his wife, Ashley, to create relationship-building resources, media, and events as part of the team at www.MarriageToday.com and www.xomarriage.com. They have four young sons and live in Keller, Texas.